Union Public Library

ARBITRARY BORDERS

Political Boundaries in World History

The Division of the Middle East
The Treaty of Sèvres

Northern Ireland and England
The Troubles

The Great Wall of China

The Green Line
The Division of Palestine

The Iron Curtain
The Cold War in Europe

The Mason–Dixon Line

Vietnam: The 17th Parallel

Korea Divided: The 38th Parallel and
the Demilitarized Zone

The U.S.–Mexico Border
The Treaty of Guadalupe Hidalgo

The Czech Republic:
The Velvet Revolution

Louisiana Territory

South Africa:
A State of Apartheid

The Partition of British India

London: From the Walled City
to New Towns

A South American Frontier:
The Tri-Border Region

China Contested:
Western Powers in East Asia

The Breakup of Yugoslavia:
Conflict in the Balkans

The Dispute Over Gibraltar

Gibraltar

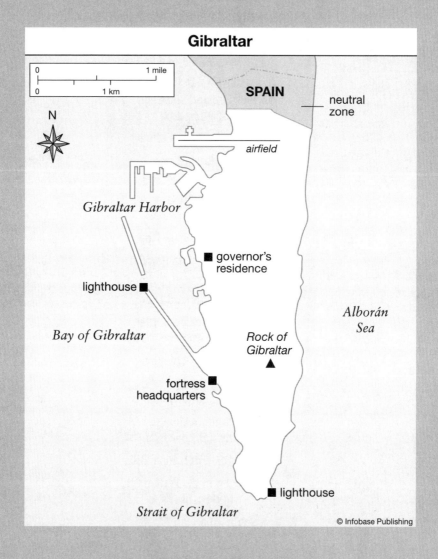

0   1 mile

0   1 km

N

SPAIN

neutral
zone

airfield

Gibraltar Harbor

■ governor's
residence

lighthouse ■

*Alborán
Sea*

Bay of Gibraltar

*Rock of
Gibraltar*
▲

fortress ■
headquarters

■ lighthouse

Strait of Gibraltar

© Infobase Publishing

The Dispute Over Gibraltar

Melissa R. Jordine

California State University, Fresno

Foreword by
Senator George J. Mitchell

Introduction by
James I. Matray
California State University, Chico

CHELSEA HOUSE
P U B L I S H E R S

An imprint of Infobase Publishing

I would like to dedicate this work to all of those individuals who supported me during its completion. This includes my colleagues at California State University, Fresno, the staff at the National Archives in London, the editors at Chelsea House, Safir Ahmed, Dr. & Ilse Detwiler, my family, my friends, and most of all Michelle DenBeste.

FRONTIS As this detailed map reveals, the British colony of Gibraltar is very small: it occupies a narrow peninsula in southern Spain that is just 3 miles long and 0.75 miles wide.

The Dispute Over Gibraltar

Copyright © 2007 by Infobase Publishing

Chelsea House
An imprint of Infobase Publishing
132 West 31st Street
New York NY 10001

Library of Congress Cataloging-in-Publication Data

Jordine, Melissa R., 1971–
    The dispute over Gibraltar / Melissa R. Jordine.
      p. cm. — (Arbitrary borders)
    Includes bibliographical references and index.
    ISBN 0-7910-8648-8 (hardcover)
      1. Gibraltar—History   2. Gibraltar—Boundaries.   3. Gibraltar—International status.   I. Title.
    DR1302.G38J67 2006
    946.8'9—dc22   2006019746

Chelsea House books are available at special discounts when purchased in bulk quantities for businesses, associations, institutions, or sales promotions. Please call our Special Sales Department in New York at (212) 967–8800 or (800) 322–8755.

You can find Chelsea House on the World Wide Web at http://www.chelseahouse.com

Text and cover design by Takeshi Takahashi

Printed in the United States of America

Bang EJB 10 9 8 7 6 5 4 3 2 1

This book is printed on acid-free paper.

All links and Web addresses were checked and verified to be correct at the time of publication. Because of the dynamic nature of the Web, some addresses and links may have changed since publication and may no longer be valid.

Contents

Foreword

Senator George J. Mitchell

I spent years working for peace in Northern Ireland and in the Middle East. I also made many visits to the Balkans during the long and violent conflict there.

Each of the three areas is unique; so is each conflict. But there are also some similarities: in each, there are differences over religion, national identity, and territory.

Deep religious differences that lead to murderous hostility are common in human history. Competing aspirations involving national identity are more recent occurrences, but often have been just as deadly.

Territorial disputes—two or more people claiming the same land—are as old as humankind. Almost without exception, such disputes have been a factor in recent conflicts. It is impossible to calculate the extent to which the demand for land—as opposed to religion, national identity, or other factors—figures in the motivation of people caught up in conflict. In my experience it is a substantial factor that has played a role in each of the three conflicts mentioned above.

In Northern Ireland and the Middle East, the location of the border was a major factor in igniting and sustaining the conflict. And it is memorialized in a dramatic and visible way: through the construction of large walls whose purpose is to physically separate the two communities.

In Belfast, the capital and largest city in Northern Ireland, the so-called "Peace Line" cuts through the heart of the city, right across urban streets. Up to thirty feet high in places, topped with barbed wire in others, it is an ugly reminder of the duration and intensity of the conflict.

In the Middle East, as I write these words, the government of Israel has embarked on a huge and controversial effort to construct a security fence roughly along the line that separates Israel from the West Bank.

Having served a tour of duty with the U.S. Army in Berlin, which was once the site of the best known of modern walls, I am skeptical of their long-term value, although they often serve short-term needs. But it cannot be said that such structures represent a new idea. Ancient China built the Great Wall to deter nomadic Mongol tribes from attacking its population.

In much the same way, other early societies established boundaries and fortified them militarily to achieve the goal of self-protection. Borders always have separated people. Indeed, that is their purpose.

This series of books examines the important and timely issue of the significance of arbitrary borders in history. Each volume focuses attention on a territorial division, but the analytical approach is more comprehensive. These studies describe arbitrary borders as places where people interact differently from the way they would if the boundary did not exist. This pattern is especially pronounced where there is no geographic reason for the boundary and no history recognizing its legitimacy. Even though many borders have been defined without legal precision, governments frequently have provided vigorous monitoring and military defense for them.

This series will show how the migration of people and exchange of goods almost always work to undermine the separation that borders seek to maintain. The continuing evolution of a European community provides a contemporary example illustrating this point, most obviously with the adoption of a single currency. Moreover, even former Soviet bloc nations have eliminated barriers to economic and political integration.

Globalization has emerged as one of the most powerful forces in international affairs during the twenty-first century. Not only have markets for the exchange of goods and services become genuinely worldwide, but instant communication and sharing of information have shattered old barriers separating people. Some scholars even argue that globalization has made the entire concept of a territorial nation-state irrelevant. Although the assertion is certainly premature and probably wrong, it highlights the importance of recognizing how borders often have reflected and affirmed the cultural, ethnic, or linguistic perimeters that define a people or a country.

Since the Cold War ended, competition over resources or a variety of interests threaten boundaries more than ever, resulting in contentious interaction, conflict, adaptation, and intermixture. How people define their borders is also a factor in determining how events develop in the surrounding region. This series will provide detailed descriptions of selected arbitrary borders in history with the objective of providing insights on how artificial boundaries separating people will influence international affairs during the next century.

Senator George J. Mitchell
September 2005

Introduction

James I. Matray
California State University, Chico

Throughout history, borders have separated people. Scholars have devoted considerable attention to assessing the significance and impact of territorial boundaries on the course of human history, explaining how they often have been sources of controversy and conflict. In the modern age, the rise of nation-states in Europe created the need for governments to negotiate treaties to confirm boundary lines that periodically changed as a consequence of wars and revolutions. European expansion in the nineteenth century imposed new borders on Africa and Asia. Many native peoples viewed these boundaries as arbitrary and, after independence, continued to contest their legitimacy. At the end of both world wars in the twentieth century, world leaders drew artificial and impermanent lines separating assorted people around the globe. Borders certainly are among the most important factors that have influenced the development of world affairs.

Chelsea House Publishers decided to publish a collection of books looking at arbitrary borders in history in response to the revival of the nuclear crisis in North Korea in October 2002. Recent tensions on the Korean peninsula are a direct consequence of Korea's partition at the 38th parallel at the end of World War II. Other nations in human history have suffered because of similar artificial divisions that have been the result of either international or domestic factors and often a combination of both. In the case of Korea, the United States and the Soviet Union decided in August 1945 to divide the country into two zones of military occupation ostensibly to facilitate the surrender of Japanese forces. However, a political contest was then underway inside Korea to determine the future of the nation after forty years of Japanese colonial rule. The Cold War then created two Koreas with sharply contrasting political, social, and economic systems that symbolized an ideological split among the Korean people. Borders separate people, but rarely prevent their economic, political, social, and cultural interaction. But in Korea, an artificial border has existed since 1945 as a nearly impenetrable barrier precluding meaningful contact between two portions of the same population. Ultimately, two authentic Koreas emerged, exposing how an arbitrary boundary can create circumstances resulting even in the permanent division of a homogeneous people in a historically united land.

Korea's experience in dealing with artificial division may well be unique, but it is not without historical parallels. The first group of books in this series on arbitrary boundaries provided description and analysis of the division of the Middle East after World War I, the Iron Curtain in Central Europe during the Cold War, the United States-Mexico Border, the 17th parallel in Vietnam, and the Mason-Dixon Line. Three authors in a second set of studies addressed the Great Wall in China, the Green Line in Israel, and the 38th parallel and demilitarized zone in Korea. Four other volumes described how discord over artificial borders in the Louisiana Territory, Northern Ireland, Czechoslovakia, and South Africa provide insights about fundamental disputes focusing on sovereignty, religion, and ethnicity. Six books now complete the series. Three authors explore the role of arbitrary boundaries in shaping the history of the city of London, the partition of British India, and the Tri-Border Region in Latin America. Finally, there are studies examining Britain's dispute with Spain over Gibraltar, Modern China, and the splintering of Yugoslavia after the end of the Cold War.

Admittedly, there are many significant differences between these boundaries, but these books will strive to cover as many common themes as possible. In so doing, each will help readers conceptualize how complex factors such as colonialism, culture, and economics determine the nature of contact between people along these borders. Although globalization has emerged as a powerful force working against the creation and maintenance of lines separating people, boundaries likely will endure as factors having a persistent influence on world events. This series of books will provide insights about the impact of arbitrary borders on human history and how such borders continue to shape the modern world.

James I. Matray
Chico, California
September 2005

1

An Extremely Bitter Dispute

The British government inaugurated Queen Elizabeth II in June 1953, and in November of that year, she set out on a tour of the British Commonwealth that was to conclude with a visit to Gibraltar on May 10–11, 1954. When the queen's itinerary was made known, the Spanish ambassador in London, Miguel Primo de Rivera, met with British Foreign Secretary Anthony Eden and requested that the visit be cancelled. The British Foreign Office in London released information about the visit, including the fact that the Spanish representative was informed that Her Majesty could not and would not alter or eliminate visits to British territory based on the protests or interests of a foreign power. Two days later, the Spanish foreign minister in Madrid issued a statement about the meeting between the British foreign secretary and the Spanish ambassador in which the issue of Gibraltar was discussed:

> It was pointed out that the Duke de Primo de Rivera had indicated the "resentment" felt by the Spanish people that "the fortress of Gibraltar" had been included in the itinerary of the Queen's Commonwealth tour and had intimated that such an event would be "imprudent," that it might have an adverse effect on Anglo-Spanish relations, and that it would inevitably call forth a "national protest" from the Spanish people given that "Gibraltar is Spanish territory to which the Spanish people do not renounce their claim."[1]

In response to the queen's visit, the Spanish government instituted border restrictions, and this led the two nations to enter into negotiations over the issues of restrictions and sovereignty. Spain tried to use the restrictions as leverage to convince the British to discuss the issue of sovereignty. Spain believed that demonstrating the vulnerability of Gibraltar and the onset of an economic depression might lead Britain to transfer the territory to Spain. Diplomats exchanged notes, and negotiations took place, but virtually no progress was made because Spain insisted that the matter of sovereignty be discussed before the

Shortly after her coronation in June 1953, Queen Elizabeth II set out on a six-month tour of the British Commonwealth. Elizabeth and her husband, Prince Philip, are pictured here at the foot of the Rock of Gibraltar on the last stop of that tour.

elimination of border restrictions; Britain insisted that discussions regarding sovereignty could not begin until the border restrictions were completely abolished. Although the Spanish actions led the British to enter into negotiations, they also reinforced anti-Spanish attitudes in Britain. Despite the economic cost of maintaining Gibraltar after Spain closed the border, the British became more determined than ever not to transfer sovereignty of "the Rock" against the wishes of the population. Thus, Spain's imposition of border restrictions actually made it less likely that Britain would cede Gibraltar to Spain. Despite the failure to resolve the key issue of sovereignty over Gibraltar, Anglo-Spanish relations actually improved between 1954 and 1980.

However, the cordial diplomatic relations between the two countries suffered a setback in 1981, when the Prince of Wales and his bride made their honeymoon plans. The British Royal couple, Charles and Diana, planned to launch their honeymoon voyage from the Bay of Gibraltar in the Royal Yacht *Britannia*. In protest, King Juan Carlos and Queen Sofia of Spain refused to attend the wedding. The British Royal couple did not change their plans, and their brief appearance in Gibraltar provoked considerable outrage in Spain.

These events illustrate the extreme bitterness that Spain continues to exhibit regarding the loss of Gibraltar, more than 300 years after the British conquest of "the Rock." Although English forces seized Gibraltar in 1704, Great Britain did not formally acquire the rights to the territory until the Treaty of Utrecht was signed in 1713. (Note: The union of Scotland, Wales, and England in 1707 created Great Britain. Therefore, although *England* is used for the earlier period, all references to this territory during and after 1707 are to *Great Britain* or *Britain*. In 1801, Great Britain became the United Kingdom of Great Britain and Ireland. An agreement reached in 1921 reduced the territory to the United Kingdom of Great Britain and Northern Ireland, and the territory adopted this name officially in 1927. However, it is the government situated in England and the population of England that are interested in and involved in the dispute over Gibraltar, and thus the terms *Britain* and *British*—instead of using U.K. after 1801— have been used throughout this work. The British maintain that they gained sovereignty over the territory when they conquered it and do not view it any differently than they do any other territorial concession gained as a result of war.

Spain insists that Great Britain was granted rights under Article X of the Treaty of Peace and Friendship (one of the agreements under the Treaty of Utrecht), but those rights are nullified if the British violate the terms of the treaty. Spain claims that only the fortress itself and no territory on land or at sea was ceded (given over), and that Gibraltar is an integral part of Spain.[2] The British disagree on both points and maintain that under the treaty, all rights were transferred absolutely to the British and all territory and territorial waters within range of the fortress guns are effectively under their jurisdiction.

Article X of the Treaty of Peace and Friendship does not establish a border or clearly indicate Spanish and British jurisdiction in regard to Gibraltar. There are actually two territories in dispute: "the Rock" itself and the isthmus or strip of land that connects Gibraltar to the Iberian Peninsula. Part of the isthmus has been occupied by England since it acquired Gibraltar, but no territory beyond the fortress and town were ceded by the treaty, and no specific border was designated.

Article X of the Treaty of Peace and Friendship clearly states that no territorial jurisdiction to the land adjacent to Gibraltar is conceded. The exact wording of the treaty, though, contributed to the difficulty in establishing a clear line of demarcation or border. "But that abuses and frauds may be avoided by importing any kinds of goods, the Catholic King wills, and takes it to be understood, that the above-named propriety be yielded to Great Britain without any territorial jurisdiction, and without any open communication by land with the country round about."[3] (The entire text of Article X appears as a sidebar article in Chapter 3.) Article X clearly suggests that the intent behind the lack of territorial jurisdiction is to prevent smuggling by stating that goods could, in times of need, be purchased from Spain for "ready money." Spain insists that only the town, fortress, and port were conceded and that the British have no right to set one foot upon the ground beyond the fortress and town.

Spain objected to the posting of sentries and other activities that occurred outside the fortress and unequivocally maintains that the airstrip built by the British during World War II, on what has been unofficially designated as "neutral ground," is on

---

Spain

La Coruna
Aviles
Santander
Bilbao
San Sebastian
Bay of Biscay
FRANCE
Gulf of Lions
Lugo
Oviedo
Gijon
Vitoria
ANDORRA
Santiago de Compostela
Leon
Miranda de Ebro
Pamplona
PYRENEES
Vigo
Orense
Ponferrada
Burgos
Logrono
Manresa
Gerona
Costa Brava
Valladolid
Duero R.
Zaragoza
Lerida
Sabadell
Zamora
Ebro R.
Reus
Barcelona
Salamanca
Alcala de Henares
Tortosa
Tarragona
Avila
Madrid
Cuenca
Gulf of Valencia
BALEARIC IS.
Minorca
PORTUGAL
Tagus R.
Toledo
Sagunto
Caceres
Valencia
Palmera
Majorca
Merida
Tomelloso
Jucar R.
Alcira
Ibiza
Badajoz
Guadiana R.
Ciudad Real
Albacete
Puertollano
Linares
Segura R.
Alicante
Andujar
Costa Blanca
Huelva
Guadalquivir R.
Cordoba
Jaen
Murcia
Mediterranean Sea
Seville
Lorca
Cartagena
Gulf of Cadiz
Utrera
Granada
Almeria
Cadiz
Malaga
Costa del Sol
Algeciras
Gibraltar **(U.K.)**
Strait of Gibraltar
Ceuta **(SPAIN)**
Melilla **(SPAIN)**
N

CANARY ISLANDS
La Palma
Lanzarote
Santa Cruz de Tenerife
Tenerife
Hierro
La Gomera
Gran Canaria
Fuerteventura
ALGERIA
MOROCCO

| 0 | 200 miles |
| 0 | 200 km |

© Infobase Publishing

This map of Spain illustrates Gibraltar's strategic importance: It lies at the tip of southern Spain, on the Strait of Gibraltar, which links the Mediterranean Sea to the Atlantic Ocean. Great Britain seized the territory from Spain in 1704 but did not formally acquire the rights to Gibraltar until the Treaty of Utrecht was signed in 1713.

Spanish territory. Britain insists that the clause prohibiting the British from exercising territorial jurisdiction (contained in the Treaty of Utrecht) enables Spanish authorities to operate in proximity to the fortress and town in order to prevent smuggling, but it does not mean that Britain has no authority outside the fortress walls. The British argue that such a strict interpretation of the clause would prevent the adequate defense of the fortress, because the British would not be able to withstand an assault by Spanish forces if these forces could dig trenches and place guns within an inch of the fortress walls.

The political and territorial (geographic) disputes over Gibraltar are therefore closely linked. In the decades after the conquest of Gibraltar, its most important function was as a base for the British Navy. The British encouraged settlement and hoped that Gibraltar could produce profits as a commercial center, but these were secondary issues. Even if Gibraltar was only a military establishment, the issue of jurisdiction on land and at sea was of vital importance. The lack of natural resources in the area required significant quantities of supplies to be sent to Gibraltar to support the garrison. If Spain turned hostile, the British had to be sure they could control the territory directly adjacent to the fortress and the waters in and near the Bay of Gibraltar, so they could protect and resupply the fortress. The Spanish view of Gibraltar as the "key to Spain," along with extreme bitterness over its loss, precluded the possibility of reaching an agreement on an official border or line of demarcation. Thus, the border has been extremely arbitrary and the British have justified their occupation—and their use of territory not ceded in the treaty—by claiming "de facto", or legal, rights.

Spain has disputed the terms of the Treaty of Utrecht (and tried to secure the return of Gibraltar by claiming that Britain violated the agreement) and argued that only Spain has jurisdiction over Gibraltar. It has refused to recognize the right of Britain to administer the territory, as demonstrated by its protest of the queen's plan to visit and the honeymoon plans of Charles and Diana. In the eyes of the Spanish, there is no border of a more arbitrary nature than the one separating Gibraltar from Spain. The idea that Gibraltar is British is firmly refuted by the

Spanish, who acknowledge only the presence and occupation of the "key to Spain" by a foreign power.

It is not just the border that is arbitrary, however. The population of Gibraltar is also, to some extent, arbitrary. Gibraltar lacks resources and opportunities, and until the eighteenth century, it was difficult to convince individuals, aside from the soldiers who were garrisoned on "the Rock," to live there permanently. In the fourteenth century, in an attempt to increase the population of the territory, King Alfonso XI of Spain issued a decree stating that swindlers, thieves, and murderers (except those who committed crimes against the Crown) could reside on Gibraltar in absolute freedom without fear of punishment or execution.[4]

The British also often tolerated individuals known to be criminals or smugglers because of the need to supply the garrison and because such individuals could be taxed. The population of Gibraltar has been in a constant state of flux, as individuals migrate to and from the territory; it was occupied by the Moors (Muslims who ruled Spain for 700 years), the Spanish, and finally, the British. The individuals who permanently settled on "the Rock" were heavily influenced by both British and Spanish customs, but the culture has changed considerably between the eighteenth and the twenty-first centuries. Spanish influence that persisted into the early half of the twentieth century has been much less noticeable since the 1940s. "Gibraltarians had more social and cultural affinity with Spain early in the century than they have today."[5] The main shopping street in Gibraltar used to reflect Spanish culture in appearance, and Spanish entertainment was readily available as late as the early twentieth century. However, beginning in the period just prior to the Spanish Civil War (1936–1939), the interaction between the population of Spain and Gibraltar decreased noticeably. The violence and brutality of the Civil War had appalled many Gibraltarians and, during the Second World War, Gibraltar was dependent upon Britain for supplies. During this period, Spanish influence was far less prominent than in previous decades. The leader of Spain,

Francisco Franco, imposed restrictions on the border between Gibraltar and Spain in the 1950s and in 1969, closed the border. The border remained closed until 1985, and by the time it was reopened, Main Street in Gibraltar had become representative of how much the colony had been strengthened by its economic and cultural ties to Great Britain. Police in British uniforms patrolled the streets, British pubs and telephone boxes were readily visible on Main Street, and the population celebrated British holidays.

Unlike Africa, India, or other territories that came under European rule, Gibraltar did not have a sizable population when it was conquered, and most of its Spanish residents fled during and after the British attack. Peter Gold, in his work on the dispute over Gibraltar, wrote that there were 4,000 people living on Gibraltar when the British took it, and only 70 stayed on.[6] In the eighteenth century, sailors were often recruited from the poorest and the most ill-reputed segments of society, and their conduct upon coming ashore after months spent below decks was notorious. In addition to destroying, pillaging, and raping, the soldiers and sailors that took Gibraltar in 1704 displayed an unusually strong anti-Catholic attitude and defiled all of the churches on Gibraltar, except the Church of St. Mary, which was defended to the last by its priest. The defilement attracted comments and attention in an age when widespread raping and looting was taken for granted as part of the spoils of war.

Most of the civilians who left Gibraltar never returned. Of those who left, most settled in the town of San Roque, overlooking the Bay of Gibraltar. These individuals not only remained within sight of "the Rock" but preserved the traditions of Spanish Gibraltar, retaining the flag and the standard that was bestowed by Queen Isabella. Because most of the Spaniards left and British, Genoese, and others settled on Gibraltar, there was soon a discernable difference between the community on Gibraltar and the Spanish community that was displaced when the British conquered it.

In the eighteenth century, however, Gibraltar was still a military garrison, and most of the inhabitants were soldiers who were ordered there by the British authorities. There was some civilian presence on Gibraltar but, as mentioned earlier, the British initially found it difficult to convince individuals to settle there permanently. Conditions on Gibraltar were less than ideal for civilians, and the area's military significance—and the frequency of sieges and assaults—further reduced its appeal. The English thought initially that even though Gibraltar was never likely to be a true colony or a source of raw materials, it might still be of value commercially and a source of profit. Queen Anne issued a decree in February 1706 that officially designated Gibraltar as a free port. The designation of Gibraltar as a free port—thus exempting all goods imported and exported from a duty or other taxes—was a deliberate attempt to increase trade. Since most European ports charged some kind of tax or fee in addition to any import or export tariffs, it would be less expensive to send goods into and out of Europe through Gibraltar so long as Gibraltar had the status of a free port.

The British government hoped that Gibraltar, situated as it was at the entrance to the Mediterranean and connected to Spain by a narrow strip of land, would become the center of considerable commercial activity, but this did not occur. The crucial obstacle to the creation of an international trading center on "the Rock" was Spain. If goods from Spain, as well as goods of other European countries transported through Spain, could be sold in Gibraltar, then trade would have flourished. Instead, a hostile Spain restricted the flow of goods into Gibraltar, even when its relations with England were relatively good. During times when Spain and England were at war, or relations were extremely strained, Spain closed the land border completely and instituted a naval blockade to prevent any supplies from reaching "the Rock." Although profits for individuals engaged in trade increased during times of crisis, so did the risk of the loss of property or life, and some merchants left when war broke out. Individuals who did not have sufficient provisions or could not help defend the fortress were often forced to relocate by the British government. Thus, the population was constantly changing because of migration and relations between England and Spain.

During periods when the two countries were friendly and there were no restrictions along the border, residents and soldiers married Spanish women who worked in Gibraltar or lived near the border. Intermarriage, which did not occur during periods when Spain and England were at war or the border was closed, often increased the population of Gibraltar and added a blend of Spanish and British influences to the local culture and traditions. When the border was open, it seemed like an artificial divide, because the economy and social life of Spain and Gibraltar were linked.

The Spanish *Reconquista*, the long process of Latin Christians wresting Iberia from the Moors between the eleventh and the fifteenth centuries, made Spain something of a frontier society in the Middle Ages—a fact which influenced its later relations with both Jews and Muslims. The culmination of the reconquest came in 1492, when Ferdinand of Aragon and Isabella of Castile, in the process of unifying Spain into a single Christian kingdom, expelled both the Jews and Muslims. Even after the expulsion of Jews and Moors from Spain, nationalism and hostility toward perceived enemies of the state continued to exert a considerable influence. The Spanish government routinely inserted a clause into treaties ceding territory, which required the nation acquiring the territory to prohibit settlement by Jews or Moors. After the English conquered Gibraltar in 1704, the population included a significant number of Jews and Moors even though the Treaty of Peace and Friendship—by which Gibraltar was ceded to Britain—did include a clause prohibiting settlement of these groups. The lack of British citizens willing to settle on the fortified limestone edifice, and the difficulty in supplying Gibraltar during periods of conflict with Spain or when the border with Spain was closed, left the British little choice but to allow Jewish and Moorish traders to settle on "the Rock." Smugglers and traders of less ill repute, able to make a ready profit, also operated on Gibraltar before and after it was acquired by England.

It was, to some extent, Spanish policy that caused the British to violate the stipulation preventing the settlement of Jews and Moors on Gibraltar. If supplies had been readily available from Spain at all times, the British would have been able to strictly enforce the clause, although this did not guarantee that they would have done so. The need to secure and maintain access to supplies and building materials led the British to negotiate a treaty with the Sultan of Morocco. The treaty, signed on July 11, 1729, stated that "the Jews and Moors, subjects of the Emperor of Morocco, shall be allowed a free traffic to buy and sell for thirty days in the city of Gibraltar and the Island of Minorca [in the Mediterannean] but not to reside in either place."[7]

It was in the interest of the Moroccan ruler to require the British to allow Jews and Moors to visit and carry out commercial transactions on Gibraltar, and these constituted a significant percentage of the civilians who remained during the "Great Siege" from 1779 to 1783. During the American War of Independence fought from 1775 until 1783, France and Spain declared war on Britain and enacted a siege of Gibraltar that was initiated in 1779. This encirclement and attack was subsequently known as the "Great Siege" in part because of the length of the siege and in part because of the large number of Spanish and French forces that participated. The American colonies achieved their independence, but the British retained control of Gibraltar. The siege lasted for 3 years, 10 months, and 12 days, but despite the deplorable conditions and severe food shortages, the British forces did not surrender. The bravery and unwillingness to surrender displayed by the forces on Gibraltar captured the imagination of the population in Britain. The British public viewed Gibraltar as a symbol of British strength and power during a crisis. After the siege, it became virtually impossible for the British government to even consider relinquishing control of the territory.

The outbreak of the French Revolution in 1789 and the Napoleonic Wars in the early nineteenth century also had an impact on Gibraltar. Napoleon banned British goods from the continent, and this act transformed Gibraltar into a key center of commerce and a base from which to smuggle British goods into continental Europe. The population of Gibraltar, and its standard of living, increased as cooperation between Spain and Britain allowed for the flow of goods and workers across the border.

After the complete defeat of Napoleon, the situation in Europe stabilized, but trade in Gibraltar decreased and so did the population. The British government, however, invested considerable money in the area, paying workers to improve defenses and to expand the dock and harbor facilities. The town began to function independently of the military garrison and was officially designated a Crown Colony in 1830.

Toward the end of the nineteenth century, the British began construction on a new naval harbor and dockyard, and replaced some of the guns on Gibraltar with more modern weapons. The introduction of guns with much greater ranges and the advent of the airplane made Gibraltar extremely vulnerable. During World War I, the population of Gibraltar did not decrease significantly as it had during previous conflicts, and cordial relations were maintained with Spain. The border remained open, and Spanish workers who had been crossing into Gibraltar to work for five decades continued to do so; Spain even provided food and other supplies to Gibraltar during the war.[8]

The interaction between the Spanish and the residents of Gibraltar demonstrated clearly that the border established on the isthmus was artificial. In the absence of a dispute over the sovereignty of Gibraltar, there was no clear and distinct division between the two territories. Despite a different system of government and a territorial border, there was a natural tendency for the two populations to interact, and strong ties existed between the two communities. During World War I, for instance, Gibraltar had closer links to Spain, which provided water and supplies, than to Britain, which was preoccupied fighting the war on the continent. During World War II, Spain had close links to Germany and Italy, against whom Great Britain was waging war.

The leader of Germany, Adolf Hitler, repeatedly and unsuccessfully attempted to secure Spain's assistance in launching an attack on the "the Rock." Great Britain evacuated more than 14,000 civilians from Gibraltar but allowed 4,000 men capable of assisting in the defense to remain. The British government carried out extensive work on a landing strip for airplanes and took other measures to improve the defenses of Gibraltar. It also allowed the territory to be used as a launching point for the Anglo-American invasion of North Africa in 1943.

At the end of World War II, the British had difficulty transporting back those individuals who had been forced to leave Gibraltar. Although some chose not to return, about 10,000 people who had been evacuated wanted to return but were unable to do so for several years because the British government could not secure enough vessels to transport them. In the decades following that war, Britain had economic problems and was under increasing pressure to decolonize dependent territories.

As mentioned previously, the British had already enacted some measures related to self-governance, including designating Gibraltar a Crown Colony in 1830, giving the population official recognition as separate from the military garrison. Britain later granted "the Rock" limited representation as a council, and several leaders of this council, such as Joshua Hassan, did not consider complete independence feasible or even desirable. The population and the Gibraltar council wanted a greater degree of autonomy and the right to make their own decisions, but they also thought it necessary to retain their links to Great Britain, even though that meant remaining a dependent territory. When Great Britain agreed to grant further autonomy to Gibraltarians, the dispute with Spain reemerged.

The dispute gained an international dimension in 1963, when Spain requested that the matter be presented before a special committee of the United Nations (UN), an international peacekeeping organization created in 1945. One of the fundamental principles stated in the UN Charter was its respect for the self-determination of all peoples. The UN established guidelines for granting independence to colonies and required colonial powers such as France and Great Britain to provide reports on all non-self-governing territories under their control. Britain considered Gibraltar to be a colony and provided reports on its status and its intention to allow greater autonomy for the territory.

Spain initially argued that, under the terms of the agreement that ceded Gibraltar to Britain, Spain had the right of first refusal should the British decide to sell or alienate Gibraltar from Great Britain in any way. When Great Britain rejected this argument and expressed its intent to grant Gibraltar a greater measure of self-governance, Spain turned to the United Nations and demanded a hearing on the matter. Spain demanded, in essence, that Gibraltar be transferred to Spanish control and annexed to Spain. Spain, however, insisted that Gibraltarians could continue to exercise authority and maintain their traditions. It seemed unusual for Spain to appeal to the UN in light of the UN commitment to decolonization, but Spain believed that, despite the anticolonial stance of the UN, it would support Spain, because Gibraltar, in Spain's view, was not a colony or true community.

Spain argued that Gibraltar was primarily a military institution and that most of its residents were displaced British citizens or disreputable traders making profits on illegal trade. In addition, because the population of Gibraltar was not an independent group that was conquered and forced to live under British rule, Spain argued, the UN resolution on self-determination did not apply. Spain successfully argued that Gibraltar did not have an indigenous population and that when England conquered it in 1704 the inhabitants were largely Spanish citizens who left as a consequence of the capture of "the Rock." Spain also pointed out that Gibraltar is part of the Iberian Peninsula, it is directly adjacent to Spain, and it had been under Spanish control between 1462 and 1704. The United Nations essentially seems to have accepted Spain's position that there was no indigenous population and that the population in the

1960s largely consisted of British military forces and British citizens who had moved there. If the population is not a true community with a legitimate claim to self-determination, then the dispute over Gibraltar should not be resolved by applying the UN resolution on self-determination. The UN committee report in reference to the situation in regard to Gibraltar only referred to UN resolution 1514 and not another resolution (1541) that also deals with decolonization. In resolution 1514 (XV), there is a specific paragraph (the sixth paragraph) stating that neither the territorial integrity nor the national unity of a nation should be disrupted.

Both Britain and Gibraltarians have rejected the Spanish argument. The population of Gibraltar was infuriated by

UN SPECIAL COMMITTEE OF 24

One of the primary aims of the United Nations was to achieve the goal of self-rule for all peoples, as stated in its charter. In the decade following World War II, some areas achieved independence, but there were still a significant number of non-self-governing territories in 1960. The UN responded to this situation by issuing the Declaration on the Granting of Independence to Colonial Countries and Peoples in that year. In 1962, the UN created the Special Committee of 24 on Decolonization, to monitor and make recommendations to implement the declaration. At Spain's insistence, the committee held a series of hearings on the status of Gibraltar. Spain argued that the territorial integrity of Spain should take precedence over the desires of the population, and Britain should deal with Spain, even if this went against the express wishes of the population.

The Special Committee did not denounce increased self-rule for Gibraltar and emphasized that the UN declaration did apply to Gibraltar. However, the official statement referred to the UN resolution on decolonization that had a detailed point indicating that the protection of the territorial integrity of nations and states should be a priority rather than mentioning the resolution on decolonization that stressed the right of the indigenous population to self-determination exclusively. The UN had found Spain's argument that Gibraltar

Spanish statements to the effect that all Gibraltarians were displaced British citizens or criminals without a unique cultural identity or traditions developed or practiced over a long period of time. By the time the UN held hearings on Gibraltar in the 1960s, the population of Gibraltar clearly had a strong sense of loyalty to and a close connection with Britain.

Britain had appropriated enormous sums of money to alleviate the economic depression that resulted from border restrictions imposed by the Spanish government that began in 1954. British influence is reflected in the laws, government, trade unions, and other aspects of life in Gibraltar. The laws reflect British traditions and codes, and the police on Gibraltar are

was not a true community but merely a British military garrison with a number of displaced British citizens compelling. The UN seemed to have rejected the Gibraltarian argument that self-determination must take precedence over all other issues, in part because abiding by the wishes of the population would force the UN to sanction or approve of Gibraltar remaining a colonial possession indefinitely.

The official UN recommendation stipulated that the dispute in regard to Gibraltar should be resolved by direct negotiation between Britain and Spain (there was no reference to Gibraltar's representatives). This put Britain in an untenable situation, since it had promised the Gibraltar council and representatives that it would not transfer sovereignty to Spain against the wishes of the population.

It is interesting to note that, in hearings before a UN committee set up to oversee the implementation of decolonization, none of the parties argued that Gibraltar should be granted independence. Spain insisted that sovereignty over Gibraltar be transferred to Spain. The UN seemed to support Spain's position when it recommended that Britain negotiate directly with Spain to end the dispute, while omitting any reference to the population. Britain and Gibraltar insisted that Gibraltar must remain under British control.

virtually indistinguishable from those in Britain. The oldest newspaper, the *Gibraltar Chronicle*, began as a British garrison newspaper. Education is set up along British lines at the secondary level, and some students complete a university degree in England. The culture of Gibraltar reflects British influence, although Spanish is also spoken and some Spanish customs persist. Leaders of the Gibraltar community acknowledge their close connection to England but insist that the town and community are separate from the military garrison and that the status of Gibraltar must be in accord with the wishes of the population.

The hearings before the UN Special Committee of 24 on Decolonization focused on the status of Gibraltar and the distinction between self-determination and complete self-rule, or independence. The United Nations supports the rights of self-determination for all people, but although Gibraltarians want greater autonomy, they insist on remaining under the control of Britain. Therefore, self-determination and political independence for Gibraltar are mutually exclusive. Alternatively, if Gibraltar were transferred to the control of Spain, it would still not become independent, but it would instead be an integral part of the Spanish nation and no longer a colonial possession.

As a result of increasing sanctions imposed by Spain, pressure from the United Nations, and the failure of Anglo-Spanish negotiations to settle the issue of Gibraltar, the British resorted to a referendum, seen by some as a radical course of action. The British prime minister announced in the House of Commons on June 14, 1967, that a referendum would be held that would ask the people of Gibraltar to vote on the following options:

1. To pass under Spanish sovereignty in accordance with the terms proposed by the Spanish Government on May 18, 1966.

2. To retain their link with Britain, with democratic local institutions and with Britain retaining its present responsibilities.[9]

Even before the vote, there was little doubt about the outcome. Transfer of Gibraltar to Spain was overwhelmingly rejected, and there was tremendous support for Britain. "'British we are and British we'll stay' read the slogan adorning the streets of Gibraltar in the colours of the Union Jack. This declaration was confirmed in a referendum held on 10 September of the same year."[10]

There were 12,237 eligible voters, and 12,138 of them voted to remain tied to Great Britain, whereas 44 voted to be transferred to the control of Spain. The British hoped the referendum would enable them to gain the support of the international community and the UN for their policies on Gibraltar, but both Spain and the UN opposed the holding of the referendum. This opposition led to an even closer relationship between the population of Gibraltar and Britain, because the majority of Gibraltarians felt they should be able to vote on their own future. Spain and the UN insisted that the matter should be resolved by direct negotiations between Spain and Britain. The vote may have been overwhelmingly pro-British, but it led to a complete impasse in Anglo-Spanish relations, and it did not gain the British any significant support from the international community.[11]

The referendum clearly reflected the attitude of the population of Gibraltar, which remains firmly tied to Britain and has rejected both a transfer to Spain and complete independence. It has been suggested that Gibraltar be annexed or come under the direct control of Britain, so the issue of sovereignty would cease to exist and Britain would have to defend it by any and all necessary means. Most individuals in both Britain and Gibraltar were and still are opposed to this option. Most Gibraltarians do not want to pay British taxes and prefer association with Britain over annexation. The British public and many British politicians have no desire to assume greater control of Gibraltar and rightly assume that the international community would protest such an action.

Spain continues to view the British possession of Gibraltar as an arbitrary separation of an integral segment of Spanish

In November 2002, 99 percent of Gibraltarians rejected a proposal that would have allowed Britain and Spain to exercise joint sovereignty over Gibraltar. Pictured here are Gibraltarians celebrating National Gibraltar Day on September 10, 2002, two months prior to the referendum to determine joint sovereignty.

territory from the mainland and has continued to dispute the exact border of the territory that was ceded to Britain. The nature and location of the border has not remained constant. It is an artificial border that has not really divided the population of the two territories, and the intermarriage and interaction between Spaniards and Gibraltarians led to a culture incorporating elements from the two territories. At times of tension and dispute between the two countries, the border has been partially or fully closed to all people, goods, and even communications and has been a real division that not only separated Gibraltar and Spain but also Britain and Spain.

The United Nations and the international community continue to be involved in the dispute over the status of Gibraltar but have been unsuccessful in resolving it. The population of Gibraltar remains anti-Spanish, and in November 2002, 99 percent of Gibraltarians rejected a proposal that would have allowed Britain and Spain to exercise joint sovereignty. New issues have emerged as the European Union has developed, and no resolution that would satisfy all concerned parties is on the horizon.[12]

Gibraltar is unusual because since 1704 it has had no official border on land or at sea, attributable to the dispute between Britain and Spain. The actual line of demarcation between the two territories, again both at land and at sea, has changed several times during the more than three centuries it has been under British control. The nature of the border and the population are also in a sense arbitrary, because neither has remained constant or unchanging for any significant length of time.

2

The Early History of Gibraltar

In the centuries prior to the creation and expansion of the Roman Empire, there was no border, arbitrary or otherwise, between Spain and Gibraltar, because no permanent settlements had been established on "the Rock." Conditions on Gibraltar were not favorable for human settlement, and those individuals who did land on Gibraltar did not remain there. In ancient times, the Phoenicians and Romans were familiar with Gibraltar but established settlements in modern-day Spain. The Iberian Peninsula was far more attractive than the barren landscape of Gibraltar, especially to cultures dependent on trade or labor-intensive agriculture for their livelihood. The Moors landed on Gibraltar in 710, and in 711 another expedition established a base there. The Moors were the first to "settle" on Gibraltar, but initially, even they used it primarily as a base from which to invade the Iberian Peninsula and were far less interested in Gibraltar itself. The border was arbitrary between 711 and 1462, because during the struggle between the Moors and Spanish leaders, Gibraltar, as well as the territory adjacent to it, changed hands several times.

In geographic terms, Gibraltar is a narrow peninsula of 2.25 square miles (5.8 square kilometers), which runs almost directly due north to south in southwestern Europe. A sandy isthmus connects Gibraltar, on its north side, to the western coast of Spain, whereas Europa Point, at the southernmost end, is approximately 20 miles (32 kilometers) from Ceuta, in Morocco, across the Strait of Gibraltar. The peninsula is a gigantic rock of Jurassic limestone, carved out over thousands of years by the wind and the sea, 1,396 feet (425.5 meters) at its highest point. The eastern face of "the Rock" is so sheer as to be virtually inaccessible. The western side gradually descends to a rocky promontory and then to a sandy stretch that provides access to a natural harbor. Gibraltar has no rivers or streams to provide drinking water and has virtually no arable land. Although the soil is not suitable for agriculture, in excess of 600 species of plants and flowers grow there. The climate is moderate, but an east wind known as the levanter, which can blow for as many as

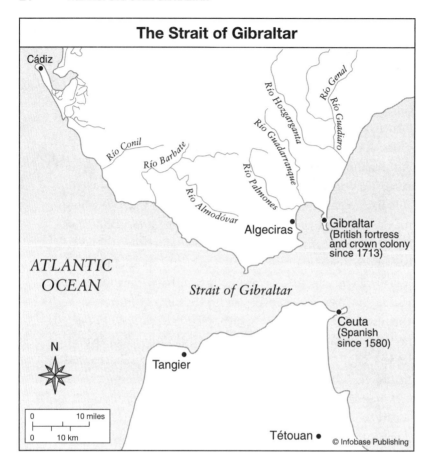

The northern end of Gibraltar is connected to Spain by a sandy isthmus, while the southern end is separated from Ceuta, a Spanish enclave in Morocco, by a 20-mile stretch of the Strait of Gibraltar. During antiquity, the entrance to the Strait of Gibraltar—the area between Gibraltar and Ceuta—was known as the Pillars of Hercules and was thought to be the western end of the world.

150 days, produces a heavy cloud cover that can lead to humidity levels of 90 percent.[13]

In ancient times, the Mediterranean Sea was the center of the known world and the Phoenicians, Greeks, and Romans all explored, traded, and established settlements along the coast. The Phoenicians were the most proficient seafaring people of the ancient world and they sailed out of the Mediterranean through the Strait of Gibraltar. Numerous legends and myths were associated with the massive limestone edifice jutting out into the Mediterranean. The Greeks, who settled on the north coast of the Mediterranean, made frequent voyages in the Aegean and Mediterranean seas. However, unlike the Phoenicians, they were unwilling to sail through the Strait of Gibraltar into the Atlantic Ocean, even issuing a warning that there was no more beyond the strait, that nothing existed on the other side.[14] This casts some light on the Greek characterization of the Atlantic Ocean as Lethe, or the waters of forgetfulness.[15] To Greek mariners, Gibraltar symbolized the end of the known world and indeed the end of civilization.[16]

Although the Phoenicians, Greeks, and Romans sailed throughout the Mediterranean, they did not establish settlements on "the Rock" itself. The Phoenicians, a Semitic-speaking people who lived along the coast of the Mediterranean Sea just to the north of Palestine and the Dead Sea, improved shipbuilding methods and established international trade routes, carrying goods long distances over the water. In 950 B.C., the Phoenicians founded Carteia (a settlement that served as an important trading outpost) on the Iberian Peninsula, about a mile from Gibraltar. (In ancient times, Gibraltar was known as Calpe or Mons Calpe. Calpe is most likely a designation derived from the Phoenician verb *Kalph*, "to hollow out."[17]) The Romans would later conquer the Phoenician settlement of Carteia and also establish a presence in modern-day Spain.

Whereas earlier people visited and settled on the Iberian Peninsula in proximity to Gibraltar, the Moors were the first to establish a settlement on "the Rock" itself. The Moors lived in Northwest Africa, in the area known today as Morocco and Mauritania. They converted to Islam in the seventh century, and in the eighth century, they used Gibraltar as a launching point for raids into Spain. In 710, when the Moorish conqueror of Maghreb (Africa, north of the Sahara), Musa ibn Nusayr, sent a small reconnaissance party from Africa across the strait,

FLAVIVS RVDERICVS

Cum Siibertus, et Eba Witizæ filij, ob eius impietatem inuisi essent,
RVDERICVS ex Theodofredo Chindaswindi Regis Nepos Rex eligitur,
et Witizæ premens uestigia, cum Iuliani Comitis filiam uiolasset, tanta
ira Patris animum Subijt, ut Saracenos in Hispaniæ perniciem ex
Africa euocare non dubitauerit. Venerunt Mauri Muza, et Tariffio
Ducibus, Hispalique oppugnata, commisso tandem certamine Ruderi-
cum profligarunt . . .

For more than 200 years (A.D. 500 to 711), the Visigoths ruled much of the Iberian Peninsula. However, by the early 700s, their power was beginning to wane, and in 711 the last Visigoth king, Roderick (depicted here), was defeated at the Battle of Guadalete by a combined force of more than 7,000 Arabs and Berbers led by Tarik ibn Ziyad.

Gibraltar was under the rule of a Visigothic king named Roderick. The expedition under the command of Tarif ibn Malik Nakli was a great success. The point where he landed was subsequently known as Tarifa, and he returned to Tangiers with the spoils of his exploits and with tales of an easy conquest.

As a result of the earlier expedition, the next year (711), Musa sent 7,000 troops across the strait under the command of Tarik ibn Ziyad. Tarik's conquest of Gibraltar and his defeat of King Roderick, in command of a much larger force, marked the beginning of Muslim rule in Gibraltar, which lasted from 711 until well into the fifteenth century.[18]

It was after this conquest that the area became known as Gibraltar. Jose Carlos de Luna indicates that, according to Ben-Hazil, the Arabs called it the Hill of Tarik, and a corrupted version of this term led to its designation as *Gibraltar*.[19] According to Ernle Bradford (in his history of Gibraltar), *Gibraltar* is an Anglicized corruption of *Gibel Tarik* (Tarik's Rock).[20] Howard Levie points out, however, that the first documented use of the term *Gibraltar* is in the Cronica de Fernando IV (1340) and states unequivocally that it is a Spanish and not an English corruption of the Arabic term, which he writes as *Djabel Tarik* ("Tarik's Rock").[21] Although historians disagree as to the exact derivation, there is no question that the term *Gibraltar* comes from the designation of the territory as Tarik's Rock.

When the extent of Tarik's victories became clear, Musa himself landed at Algeciras, in April 712, with a force of 18,000 troops, and before he was recalled to Damascus by the caliph in 714, the conquest of Spain was all but complete.[22] In reality, the Muslim invasion and victory in battle against the Visigoths and then the Spanish was not the end of an independent Spain but rather just the beginning of a struggle between the Moors and the Christian princes for control of the territory. Moorish and Christian kingdoms (independent territories or entities) on the Iberian Peninsula were established, were conquered, disappeared, and passed from Spanish to Moorish or Moorish to Spanish control during the eighth, ninth, and tenth centuries.

In 1160, the leader of the Almohades, Abd-al-mu'min, initiated a construction project on "the Rock." The Almohades were a Muslim faction from Africa that believed that the Almoravids, the Muslim dynasty ruling in Spain, had strayed from the true path. In addition to defeating the Almoravids and occupying

Gibraltar, the Almohades also renamed the area *Djabel al-Fath* ("the rock of victory"), in honor of their victory.[23] This name never replaced the original designation of Djabel Tarik, however, and in a relatively brief period it disappeared altogether from the Arabic language. Although the Moors erected some fortifications and buildings, the construction necessary to carry out the original plan was never completed. Remnants of the buildings constructed and inhabited by the Moors can still be seen in Gibraltar. The Moors did build a mosque and a system to collect and store rainwater, though, and they also began building a massive wall.[24]

Although the Moors were the first to "settle" on Gibraltar, the settlement was a military base. Even soldiers in the army preferred to leave Gibraltar and participate in raids on the Iberian Peninsula, where they could plunder and lay claim to valuable land. The conquest of Gibraltar, when it was under the control of a Muslim force, the Almohades faction, demonstrates the fragmentation of the Muslim empire and the rivalry that existed between different Muslim factions or kingdoms. More than one Muslim state was established in modern-day Spain, and these states fought against each other as well as against the Christian kingdoms. Even as late as the fourteenth century, there was no real community or civilian population living on Gibraltar. There was also no official or permanent border between Gibraltar and the mainland Iberian Peninsula during this period. The territory adjacent to Gibraltar was alternately occupied by Spanish and Moorish armies; between 1309 and 1462, the Rock of Gibraltar was besieged eight times and changed hands four times. Spanish forces retook Gibraltar in 1462, and it remained under Spanish control until the British seized it in 1704. The Moors occupied southern Spain and Gibraltar for 750 years, and their final defeat would come to signify the unification and emergence of a powerful Spain. The struggle to take Gibraltar from the Moors made a lasting impression on the Spanish.

The Duke of Medina Sidonia, Alonso Perez de Guzman, claimed Gibraltar as part of his personal fiefdom, a claim

Iberian Peninsula, 910

Bay of Biscay

KINGDOM OF NAVARRE

Galicia

Asturias

León

Pamplona

Frankish enclaves

COUNTY OF BARCELONA

KINGDOM OF LEÓN

Castile

Ebro R.

Barcelona

Douro R.

UMAYYAD EMIRATE OF CORDOBA

BALEARIC IS.

Toledo

Tagus R.

Lisbon

Guadiana R.

Córdoba

Guadalquivir R.

Murcia

Mediterranean Sea

Granada

Cadiz

ATLANTIC OCEAN

N

| 0 | 120 miles |
| 0 | 120 km |

© Infobase Publishing

The Moors, who came from North Africa, ruled the majority of the Iberian Peninsula from A.D. 711 to the early thirteenth century. However, the Moorish kingdom of Granada reigned in southern Spain for another three centuries before Spanish Christians drove the Moors from the peninsula in 1492. This map illustrates the extent of Moorish holdings on the Iberian Peninsula in the early tenth century.

ignored by King Henry IV of Castile, who annexed it in the name of the Crown. Gibraltar came under the rule of the Duke of Medina Sidonia's son after another siege, the ninth one, in 1467. As of that year, territorial jurisdiction over Gibraltar, in perpetuity, was formally granted to the duke's family and it was under their patronage that the development of Gibraltar was greatly enhanced. The fortifications were improved, and both a naval base and port and a cooperage industry (which made wooden casks or tubs) were established.[25] During this period, the Gibraltar shipyards built and maintained the Spanish fleet, and both the shipyards and the town were extremely prosperous.[26] The dispute between the duke and the Crown with regard to the status of Gibraltar is significant because if Gibraltar is a Crown possession, it is part of Spain, whereas if it is under the control of an individual, it would be a separate territory with a border. No official border between "the Rock" and the mainland Iberian Peninsula was designated in the fourteenth century, or indeed ever.

The marriage of Ferdinand of Aragon and Isabella of Castille, in 1469, would prove to be a significant event for both Spain and Gibraltar. The Duke of Medina Sidonia supported Ferdinand and Isabella in their campaign against the Moors, who continued to occupy the kingdom of Granada. The Moors were defeated and driven from Spain in 1492, and the Duke of Medina Sidonia was granted the title of Marquis of Gibraltar. Nevertheless, the Crown retained an interest in Gibraltar and was finally able to gain control over the area in 1502, when it was incorporated within the domains of the Spanish Crown and granted its own coat of arms, a castle with a golden key pendant. In 1624, the Spanish king, Philip IV, visited Gibraltar and ordered the construction of even more extensive fortifications, including walls and ditches, and these defenses, together with the cannons that had already been installed, made Gibraltar nearly impregnable as a fortress.

Unfortunately, the strength of Gibraltar depended not just on the maintenance of its defenses but also on its stores of food and water, because almost all supplies had to be brought in, especially in times of siege. Bringing in supplies by land or sea was not the only difficulty faced by those in possession of "the Rock." The Spanish Crown had an exceedingly difficult time convincing individuals to live on Gibraltar. A charter issued by King Ferdinand of Spain in 1310 foreshadows later patterns of settlement. It grants a pardon to any criminals willing to live on Gibraltar, except those who committed a crime against the king or the state. The Spanish king was determined to attract a Christian population, but the morality of the inhabitants was not of any particular interest. Whenever troops were stationed on Gibraltar, their presence attracted traders and others willing to live and work in the settlement at the base of the fortress. Smugglers, more legitimate traders, criminals, and the poorer inhabitants of Spain gravitated to Gibraltar.

By 1704, after the outbreak of the War of the Spanish Succession, the series of wars and sieges that had been fought to secure Gibraltar for the Spanish Crown were long forgotten. Extensive construction and fortifications had been carried out by this time, under the various forces that occupied Gibraltar. The last major assault against "the Rock" had occurred more than 200 years earlier, and the population had increased. The town was more prosperous, trade had increased, and farmers grew additional agricultural produce on the fertile plain that lay between "the Rock" itself and Spain. There was no border between Gibraltar and the Iberian Peninsula, as long as Gibraltar was a Spanish possession.

By 1704, the long period of peace and the relative security of Spain resulted in the deterioration of the fortress and defenses on Gibraltar. The governor of Gibraltar, General Diego de Salinas, had complained about the inadequacies of the small number of troops in his garrison and the shortage of cannons and ammunition to his superiors, but to no avail.

The conquest of Gibraltar by the British in 1704 has been characterized as an "accident" rather than a premeditated action based on the perceived value of "the Rock." Although the latter part of the statement is definitely true, it was not an accident so much as a consequence of coalition warfare and the combined impact of unforeseen events. Sir George Rooke, commander of the grand fleet in the Mediterranean, was one of the first British career naval officers and a Tory (a member of Britain's Conservative Party). Rooke was ordered to support Charles III,

(*continued on page 34*)

THE WAR OF THE SPANISH SUCCESSION

The king of France, Louis XIV (1643–1715), aggressively pursued the expansion of French territory and power. He recognized that an alliance with Spain would greatly enhance the power and status of France and attempted to create a situation in which he might influence or dominate the ruler of Spain. In 1659, Louis XIV agreed to marry Maria Teresa, who was the eldest daughter of King Philip IV of Spain. The marriage contract stipulated that both Louis XIV and Maria Teresa renounce any and all claims upon the Spanish Crown, and it required Spain to pay a large dowry in return for the French renunciation of any claims to the Spanish throne. Louis XIV was not able to immediately exert any influence on the Spanish succession, and Charles II became the king of Spain. Louis XIV was not discouraged, though, and by keeping up constant diplomatic pressure, he succeeded in convincing the Spanish to select a French candidate to succeed Charles II. Upon the death of Charles II in November of 1700, Louis's grandson Philip, the Duke of Anjou, was proclaimed King Philip V of Spain. Louis XIV argued that the election of Philip did not violate the marriage contract, because it had already been nullified by the failure of Spain to finish paying the dowry.

Other European powers were adamantly opposed to the increase of France's power and influence and to the ascension of a French candidate to the Spanish throne. A Grand Alliance was formed on September 7, 1701, and war broke out. The members of the Grand Alliance, which consisted of the Habsburg Empire, England, the Netherlands, Brandenburg Prussia, as well as several additional German states, went to war against France, Spain, Savoy, Mantua, Bavaria, and Cologne. The War of Spanish Succession was fought between 1702 and 1713 in Europe and the colonial empires in North America. The war was fought mainly in the Low Countries (what is today the Netherlands, Belgium, and Luxembourg) and Germany.

By 1704, the Franco-Bavarian forces were strong enough to undertake preparations to invade Austria and conquer Vienna, but the Grand Alliance was determined to prevent the French from doing so. The Alliance also planned to defeat and expel the French forces from Germany. The taking of Gibraltar by an Anglo-Dutch fleet in 1704 was quickly overshadowed by the crushing blow dealt to the French Army at Blenheim. The victory at Blenheim eliminated the threat of a French invasion of Austria and also forced the French to withdraw from Germany. The war officially came to an end with the signing of the treaties of Utrecht in 1713 and Rastatt in 1714. Despite the victory of the Grand Alliance, Philip V was confirmed as the ruler of Spain, and the Bourbon Dynasty continued to rule Spain into the twentieth century. The Allies had achieved their main aim, because the treaty stipulated that the thrones of France and Spain must remain separate, and the war had weakened both countries. The Spanish Netherlands, Milan, and Naples were given to Austria, and Brandenburg Prussia also gained territory from the defeated nations. England perhaps gained the most as a result of the war; in addition to Gibraltar, which soon became the most disputed and visible British acquisition, Britain emerged from the conflict with the most powerful navy and was able to maintain its trading network and thus sustain its growing economy.

The War of the Spanish Succession is a good example of coalition warfare in a century in which European countries were still concerned with power and expansion in Europe, even as they simultaneously struggled to establish and maintain empires overseas. Britain and her allies agreed to allow Philip V to become the king of Spain, despite having gone to war to prevent this succession, partly in exchange for a guarantee that the Spanish and French states would not be merged, and partly because by the end of the war the possibility of French domination of Europe seemed far less likely.

Although the larger issue of rule in Europe was resolved by the British and her allies, at least temporarily, other issues, such as control of the seas and competition for markets and colonies, were not resolved, however. The British demand for Gibraltar had less to do with acquiring territory than with setting up military bases that would allow the British Navy to support and protect British trade and overseas possessions. These larger issues affected the negotiations ending the War of Spanish Succession and the terms under which Gibraltar was ceded to the British. The division between Spain and Gibraltar became a reality upon the conquest of Gibraltar by the British in 1704, but the border remained arbitrary in nature even after the signing of the Peace Treaty in 1713. The border has remained arbitrary in nature to the present day.

(*continued from page 31*)

the Austrian claimant to the throne, and had participated in a landing at Barcelona, where the population was supposed to rise up and support Charles III. That did not happen, and because the landing party was not large enough to undertake a real siege, Rooke and Prince Hesse, who was Charles III's commander in chief, were forced to withdraw.

The incident lowered the morale of all parties involved, and following this debacle, Rooke pursued a French fleet for some distance before withdrawing without contact, because of the condition of his own ships and the absence of favorable winds.[27] Rooke was then advised to attack Cadiz, just to the northwest of Gibraltar, but he was convinced it would be a disaster. At this juncture, Rooke desperately needed to take some kind of decisive action so that his career would not be ruined. The weaknesses of Gibraltar were well known, and before sailing from Portugal, Rooke had obtained a letter from Charles III demanding that Gibraltar surrender. Rooke called a council of war, where it was agreed that the attack on Cadiz was unfeasible. Rooke, and the other members of the council, also agreed that the seizure of Gibraltar would enable the Allies to monitor and control the entrance to the Mediterranean and might cause the Spanish to enter into negotiations to end the war.

The Spanish governor, General Diego de Salinas, did not have adequate forces, provisions, or cannons but was determined to resist the British, or at least to delay the seizure of Gibraltar, because it could be used to launch an attack into Spain. Rooke sent the letter from Charles III demanding the surrender of the fortress to his allies and requested a response. Salinas and the Gibraltarians responded that, having sworn an oath to Philip V, they were not in any way under the authority of Charles III.[28] General Salinas upheld his duty by trying to defend Gibraltar despite his lack of resources, but defeat was rapid and inevitable.

Rooke delayed his attack slightly because of unfavorable winds, but as soon as he was able to get his ships into position, he fired shells into the town of Gibraltar as well as at the fortress.

The Raising of the Siege of Gibraltar by Sir John Leake depicts the English conquest of Gibraltar during the War of the Spanish Succession in 1704. A combined English and Dutch fleet, led by Admiral Sir George Rooke, captured "the Rock" after a six-hour bombardment.

Salinas and his meager forces could not prevent the landing of British forces on "the Rock." The Spanish, however, did set off an explosion in one of the forts from which they had retreated after the guns were shattered. Forty British troops were killed in the explosion, 60 others were wounded, and 7 of the landing boats were capsized. Since the landings had made the Spanish position untenable, negotiations for the surrender of the fortress commenced. General Salinas and his soldiers were allowed to march out of the fort with their possessions and return to Spain.[29]

Most of the Spanish population of Gibraltar fled to Spain, as well. The miserable and unhealthy conditions on naval vessels, as well as the unsavory character of most men pressed into military service in the eighteenth century, were well known. Nevertheless, the actions of the drunken British forces, who raped women, pillaged the town for anything of value, and took delight in defiling and destroying eighteen of the nineteen Roman Catholic churches, were characterized as excessive even by the standards of the day and left lingering resentments.[30]

Some accounts suggest that Rooke participated in the ceremony that proclaimed Gibraltar had been ceded to Charles III but immediately after the ceremony claimed possession of Gibraltar for Queen Anne of England and replaced Charles III's flag with the British Union Jack flag.[31] This story, considered by most scholars who have written about Gibraltar to be a myth, has been traced back as far as Lopez de Ayala, who wrote about Gibraltar in 1782. Ayala, however, does not indicate where he obtained his information.[32] Considerable evidence suggests that, when Gibraltar was occupied, the individuals involved acted not to secure "the Rock" for Queen Anne of England but only "to reduce Gibraltar to the King of Spain's obedience."[33] Nevertheless, England had provided the bulk of the ships and the men that captured Gibraltar, and unless they allotted forces to defend it against the inevitable counterattack, it could not have been held.

The unexpected acquisition of Gibraltar led to a debate in England over whether Gibraltar should be returned to Spain. The Spanish began to assemble forces to divest the "key to Spain" of the occupying forces. By September, they had 4,000 troops, and by October, they had 7,000 assembled and camped out just beyond range of the cannons on Gibraltar. Rooke improved the defenses of Gibraltar and secured enough supplies and reinforcements to hold out against the French and Spanish. Queen Anne authorized the reinforcement of Gibraltar, and the French and Spanish were unable to effectively coordinate their efforts against the fortress.

If Gibraltar had fallen before negotiations to end the War of the Spanish Succession, the British would have in all likelihood not have demanded that it be ceded to Britain. After all, although British opinion on the value of Gibraltar was divided, Spain considered Gibraltar to be of the utmost importance and would have been in a much stronger position if it had control of Gibraltar when the war ended. The Spanish, however, failed to

After the English captured Gibraltar in 1704, Admiral Sir George Rooke became military governor of "the Rock." Rooke quickly worked to improve Gibraltar's defenses by bringing in reinforcements and supplies, which enabled the terri- tory to withstand attacks by Franco-Spanish forces over the next nine years.

take back Gibraltar between 1704 and 1711, when negotiations to end the War of the Spanish Succession began in earnest. This failure would become more significant as the decades passed, and over time, it appeared less and less likely that Gibraltar would be returned to Spain, even if another valuable territory were offered in exchange.

The British had opened negotiations with Louis XIV in secret and resolved the matter of Gibraltar and Minorca without consulting their Dutch allies. The British realized the advantages of not consulting their allies, who were unable to continue the war without Britain's support, a fact they acknowledged when the secret negotiations became public. These early negotiations were important because they influenced the terms of the Treaty of Utrecht.[34]

Louis XIV obtained permission from his grandson Philip V of Spain to negotiate on his behalf. By the end of the war, the idea of allowing Gibraltar to return to Spain in exchange for alternate concessions was not a viable option, for several reasons: (1) Gibraltar was clearly of value to Britain because of its position overlooking the strait; (2) Britain was in a position to demand both Gibraltar and Port Mahon (on Minorca); and (3) although Spain greatly desired the return of "the Rock," it was Louis XIV of France who negotiated with the British. At first, Britain stated that Port Mahon and Gibraltar itself must be ceded, but subsequently increased its demands: The British, in a letter to Louis XIV, requested "that an extent of country round Gibraltar equal to two cannon shot, and the whole island of Minorca be ceded to England."[35] Louis XIV wrote the following in response:

> [T]he King had great difficulty to induce the King of Spain to give up Gibraltar to the English, that Prince's intention being, as he often declared, not to yield an inch of land in Spain. It will be still much more difficult to obtain from him the smallest concession, on so important a point now, when he is urged to renounce his rights to the Crown of France, and look upon Spain as the only patrimony he can leave to his descendants. So that this new demand will be sure of a refusal, and the power which His Majesty [Louis XIV] has received from the Catholic King [Philip V of Spain] is directly contrary to such

a pretension. As he [Philip V] has not explained himself with regard to the entire cession of Minorca, the King [Louis XIV] will use his endeavors to obtain it, as a sort of equivalent for territory round Gibraltar; and on this consideration, and from this time, His Majesty [Louis XIV] promises that the whole island of Minorca shall be ceded.[36]

Several key issues of the War of the Spanish Succession, such as trading concessions to the British and the question of Minorca, were eventually settled and the written articles formalizing these agreements drawn up without any difficulty. The clause dealing with Gibraltar, however, provoked considerable debate, and virtually every phrase was disputed. Despite the time and effort invested in drafting Article X ceding Gibraltar, the wording was vague, and it failed to provide specific details on the exact border, sowing the seeds of a border dispute that would last into the twenty-first century. Spain's unwillingness to agree to a border was understandable, given the circumstances. Because Philip V did not have an alternative, he ceded Gibraltar, but it was in Spain's interest to interpret the territorial concession in the strictest manner. Spain used the dispute over jurisdiction on land and at sea to harass the British and to emphasize the vulnerability of Gibraltar as a naval base.

Although the Spanish position is relatively clear, the British willingness to agree to a treaty that did not designate specific boundaries is more difficult to understand. Of course, the British did not know in 1713 that Spain would attempt to use the lack of a precise border, such as the 38th parallel established in Korea, to nullify the transfer of sovereignty over Gibraltar. Furthermore, the British had to negotiate with Louis XIV and Philip V, while also dealing with the Dutch, who had fought on their side. The British were also furthering their own interests by insisting upon their right to all territory within a distance of "two cannon shot" around the fortress of Gibraltar. British demands for territorial concessions were unprecedented, were not supported by previous international agreements, and were

rejected by Louis XIV. The British were also negotiating without the full support of their allies and thus could not afford for negotiations to drag on for an extended period of time. These issues, and the fact that Britain controlled the territory adjacent to Gibraltar during the negotiations, made it more desirable in the short term to avoid designating an official line of demarcation. After all, during the negotiations that resulted in Spain ceding Gibraltar, the British occupied more territory than was likely to be ceded under the terms of the treaty.

The failure of Britain to obtain a specific agreement on the boundary is also partly explained by the fact that several leading British diplomats favored returning Gibraltar to Spain. It was understood that Gibraltar would be retained until a time when the return of Gibraltar could be used to gain a more valuable territory or the support of Spain in a crucial situation, but the permanent retention of Gibraltar was inconceivable to individuals such as Lord James Stanhope. Stanhope was made a viscount in 1717, served as King George I's principal minister in 1718, and was the British secretary of state in 1721, when the issue of Gibraltar came up again.

Stanhope offered to return Gibraltar to Spain in 1718 on the condition that Spain give up all claims to Italian territory. Before this offer was voted on by the British Parliament, however, Britain defeated Spain in a naval battle, and it looked as though the matter would be dropped. Consequently, Spain attempted to bribe British officials to both raise the issue and to vote in favor of returning Gibraltar to Spain. When it became clear that the British Parliament was unwilling to even consider the issue, Spain responded by failing to sign the necessary annual permits that gave Britain the right to conduct the slave trade in Spanish overseas possessions, including the Spanish Indies.

Stanhope secretly promised to obtain the cession of Gibraltar, and his influence led George I to send a letter to the king of Spain promising to return Gibraltar at the first opportunity and with the consent of Parliament. The king of Spain immediately signed the permits, but when the restoration of

Gibraltar did not follow, a dispute emerged about what had actually been promised by the British monarch. This chain of events suggests that the king and his ministers considered Gibraltar to be of more value as a bargaining chip than as a possession. Unfortunately, the public and some parliamentary representatives did not agree, and thus Gibraltar was not transferred to Spanish control.

The possibility that Gibraltar would be returned to Spain made it less necessary to establish a clear border. Furthermore, the division of opinion in Britain and the extensive debates in Parliament and commentary by the public when issues relating to Gibraltar were raised made avoiding the issue whenever possible an appealing option. The border was clearly arbitrary during this period: There was no official line of demarcation, the British and Spanish forces shifted position, and interaction among the British garrison, the few civilians living on Gibraltar, and the Spanish did not remain consistent in the first several decades of the eighteenth century.

The British, however, were simply not unduly concerned about the arbitrary nature of the border between Gibraltar and Spain, at the beginning of the eighteenth century. British forces were occupying sufficient territory outside the fortress, despite the fact that this area was not officially ceded to Britain, in order to be able to defend "the Rock," and there was not a sizable civilian population that might have pressed for control of a greater amount of territory outside the fortress. Britain's primary worry was about securing supplies and maintaining its forces on Gibraltar, in the event that Spain turned hostile.

3

The "Gibraltar Tradition"

As a result of meetings held July 2–13, 1713, Britain formally acquired Gibraltar under the terms of Article X of the Treaty of Peace and Friendship signed at Utrecht. Before the ink dried on the treaty, however, disputes over borders and jurisdictions emerged. The Dutch, who had participated in the taking of Gibraltar, as well as in the general war effort, made it clear that they expected to benefit directly if any territories were ceded. The British undertook secret negotiations with the French but could not keep these attempts at peace from their allies. The Dutch refused to remove their forces from Gibraltar, they denounced the British discussions with Louis XIV, and they threatened to continue the war. Eventually, the Dutch, who needed British support to secure their own border from future French aggression, accepted the agreements that Britain had secured.

Some British ministers were increasingly concerned that these agreements were being made without the participation of Philip V or Spain, even though Philip V had given his grandfather Louis XIV permission to negotiate on his behalf. The British have insisted, during the negotiations to end the War of the Spanish Succession and up to the present day, that they acquired Gibraltar by conquering it and not as a result of the treaty signed by the king of Spain. According to the British, because their forces already occupied the fortress when the treaty was written and signed, the king of Spain no longer held the territory and therefore could not transfer the rights to it. One reason Philip V agreed to an article formally ceding Gibraltar was because the British already held it by force. Moreover, by formally ceding it, he might be able to impose certain conditions on British control of Gibraltar. Also, despite signing a treaty ceding all manner of rights forever, all parties understood that in practical terms *forever* really meant until or unless Spain had the opportunity to recover Gibraltar.

The question of exactly what territory would be ceded was raised before the signing of the Treaty of Utrecht. As mentioned previously, Britain, in its letter to Louis XIV, had requested "une

King Philip V ruled Spain from 1700 to 1746 but was defeated during the War of the Spanish Succession and forced to cede all Spanish territories outside of Spain. In addition, he had to agree to the terms of Article X of the Treaty of Utrecht, which ceded Gibraltar to Great Britain.

etendue de terre de deux portees de cannon" (an extent of country equal to two cannon shots).[37] The British wanted to set a new precedent in international law that would give the country acquiring a new territory the right to the land and/or sea around it equal to twice the distance that a cannon could fire. How far a cannon could fire, however, depended on the elevation of the gun, as well as on a great many other factors, and ranged from 500 to 4,000 meters.

Although Louis XIV was quite willing to make peace in exchange for territory, he was unwilling to set a precedent that could have repercussions for France. Louis XIV professed he was unable to grant rights to the territory around Gibraltar, saying that would have to be settled by an agreement between Spain and Britain. The British negotiated directly with representatives of Philip V to draft Article X of the Treaty of Peace and Friendship.

Extended negotiations were necessary to draft Article X. Despite the time and effort spent in drafting this article, several of the conditions were somewhat vague and readily open to more than one interpretation. The unclear wording of some of the provisions, Spain's ongoing determination to recover Gibraltar, and the divided opinions within Britain on retaining or returning Gibraltar created the conditions that have led to the 300-year dispute over Gibraltar. Since the Treaty of Utrecht was signed, Spain has attempted to recover Gibraltar by force, through diplomatic negotiation, and by arguing that the British have violated the terms of the treaty, thus invalidating its right to Gibraltar. Spain, however, has never directly challenged the concept that the British took Gibraltar by force.

One factor that emerged after the signing of the Treaty of Peace and Friendship was the failure of Article X to designate an exact border or line of demarcation. The British had occupied the whole of the isthmus between Spain and Gibraltar and were not inclined to give up through negotiation what they had taken by force. The Spanish, bitter at the loss of Gibraltar, insisted that

> the Governor of Gibraltar was not to have a greater jurisdiction than before, nor an inch of ground beyond what is contained within his walls, nor any free intercourse otherwise than by sea . . . he was to have none by land other than a good

correspondence, and liberty to walk abroad by way of refreshment, and to receive such provision as he should desire and have need of.[38]

The British withdrew their outposts from much of the isthmus, but two forward positions were maintained, and whenever the Spanish attempted to erect lines of defense within the disputed territory, they were challenged by the British. A series of letters between the two countries make it very clear that Spain adamantly insists that the fortress and town of Gibraltar were the only territories ceded.[39]

ARTICLE X OF THE TREATY OF PEACE AND FRIENDSHIP

Under the terms of the 1713 Treaty of Utrecht, which brought the War of the Spanish Succession to a close, Britain formally acquired the rights to Gibraltar from Spain. The excerpt that follows is from Article X of the treaty, which spells out the terms of the transfer.

The Catholic King does hereby, for himself, his heirs and successors, yield to the Crown of Great Britain the full and entire propriety of the Town and Castle of Gibraltar, together with the port, fortifications, and forts thereunto belonging; and He gives up the said propriety, to be held and enjoyed absolutely with all manner of right for ever, without any exception or impediment whatsoever. But that abuses and frauds may be avoided by importing any kinds of goods, the Catholic King wills, and takes it to be understood, that the above-named propriety be yielded to Great Britain without any territorial jurisdiction, and without any open communication by land with the country round about. Yet whereas the communication by sea with the coast of Spain may not at all times be safe or open, and thereby it may happen that the garrison, and other inhabitants of Gibraltar may be brought to great strait; and as it is the intention of the Catholic King, only that fraudulent importation of goods should, as is above said, be hindered by an inland communication, it is therefore provided that in such cases it may be lawful to purchase, for ready money, in the neighboring territories of

Although Spain considered Gibraltar to be of great value, British governments in the eighteenth century viewed it quite differently. The British, partly because of the cost of maintaining Gibraltar and partly because of its vulnerability to blockades and sieges by Spain, considered it to be of more value as a bargaining chip than as a territory. This view is clearly demonstrated by the fact that the British made at least seven attempts to return Gibraltar to Spain in exchange for specific concessions in the first 15 years after the Treaty of Utrecht was signed.[40]

The death of Louis XIV in 1715, and the agreement between France and Spain prohibiting any claim by Philip V on

Spain, provisions, and other things necessary for the use of the garrison, the inhabitants and the ships which lie in the harbor. But if any goods be found imported by Gibraltar, either by way of barter for purchasing provisions, or under any other pretence, the same shall be confiscated, and complaint being made thereof, those persons who have acted contrary to the faith of the Treaty shall be severely punished. And her Britannic Majesty, at the request of the Catholic King, does consent and agree, that no leave shall be given under any pretence whatsoever, either to Jew or Moors, to reside or have their dwellings in the said town of Gibraltar; and that no refuge or shelter shall be allowed to any Moorish ships of war in the harbor of the said town, whereby the communication between Spain and Ceuta may be obstructed, or the coasts of Spain be infested by the excursions of the Moors. But whereas Treaties of friendship, and a liberty and intercourse of commerce are between the British and certain territories situate on the coast of Africa, it is always to be understood, that the free exercise of their religion shall be indulged to the Roman Catholic inhabitants of the aforesaid town. And in case it shall hereafter seem meet to the Crown of Great Britain to grant, sell, or by any means to alienate therefrom the propriety of said town of Gibraltar, it is hereby agreed and concluded, that the preference of having the same shall always be given to the Crown of Spain before any others.*

* George Hills, *Rock of Contention: A History of Gibraltar.* London: Robert Hale and Company, 1974, pp. 222–223.

This broadsheet, or newspaper, depicts various scenes leading up to the signing of the Treaty of Utrecht in 1713. During the first 15 years that the British held Gibraltar, they mainly used it as a bargaining chip to acquire other lands from Spain. The Spanish, however, apparently did not hold Gibraltar's strategic importance in high regard, because they turned down seven attempts by the British to return "the Rock."

the French monarchy, together with Spain's frustration over losing Gibraltar, led to British concern that another war would break out. Britain was successful in convincing France, Austria, and after some time, Holland, to join what became the Quadruple Alliance. If peace was the goal, however, it would be necessary to convince Spain to join the alliance. George I became the British monarch in 1714, and Britain's foreign policy was carried out by General James Stanhope, who attempted to gain Spanish cooperation with a promise to restore Gibraltar to them. Since the British public and Parliament would likely object to the return of Gibraltar, the negotiations were carried out in secret, but the British representative was never able to meet with Philip V, and so the first attempt to use Gibraltar as a bargaining chip failed.

After Spanish forces conquered the island of Sardinia in 1717, Stanhope gave the British ambassador in Madrid permission to offer Gibraltar to Spain to prevent further Spanish campaigns and thus preserve peace. This offer was made in secrecy, although the French ambassador in Madrid confirmed the offer on behalf of the Duke of Orleans, who had been named regent of France when Louis XIV died. Spain's ambitious chief minister, Cardinal Alberoni, was more interested in Italian territory than in Gibraltar, and rejected the offer. Stanhope warned Alberoni that Britain would go to war if Spain launched an attack against Sicily or Naples.

In a battle on August 11, 1718, Admiral George Byng destroyed the Spanish fleet, isolating the Spanish expeditionary force in Sicily. By the end of the week, Austria joined the Quadruple Alliance and the three nations declared war on Spain later that year. The first attempts to trade Gibraltar for more valuable territory were not fruitful. After further French victories in Spain, Alberoni was replaced, and, in 1720, Philip V had no choice but to agree to peace. Before signing the Treaty of Madrid, which formally established an alliance between Spain, France, and Britain, Philip raised the question of the return of Gibraltar. Stanhope wrote the following letter to the minister in Madrid explaining the current situation in Britain with regard to Gibraltar:

> We have made a motion relative to the restitution of Gibraltar, to pass a bill for the purpose of leaving the King the power of disposing of that fortress for the advantage of his subjects. You cannot imagine the ferment which the proposal produced. The public was roused with indignation at the simple suspicion that at the close of a successful war, so unjustly begun by Cardinal Alberoni, we should cede that fortress. . . . We were accordingly compelled to yield to the torrent, and to adopt the wise resolution of withdrawing the motion;

because, if it had been pressed, it would have produced the contrary effect to what is designed, and would perhaps have ended in a bill which might for ever have tied up the King's hands. Such being the real state of this business you will endeavor to explain to the Court of Madrid that if the King of Spain should ever wish, at some future day, to treat concerning the cession of Gibraltar, the only method of succeeding would be to drop the matter.[41]

Stanhope hoped to exploit the very great esteem in which Spain held Gibraltar by trading it for a territory with greater natural resources and strategic value. Britain, he thought, could profit considerably by offering to return Gibraltar to Spain. He felt that issues of nationalism and prestige would far outweigh any practical considerations. The Spanish king would not agree to concessions and was completely outraged when the Treaty of Madrid, signed in 1721, did not make any reference to the territory. He demanded that the new British minister, Charles Townshend, request a letter from the British king addressing the issue of Gibraltar.

Townshend was also one of the individuals whom King George I consulted prior to sending two letters to the king of Spain. The British monarch promised to take the first opportunity to address the issue of the return of Gibraltar, with the consent of his Parliament. The first letter requested that Spain provide an equivalent territory in exchange for Gibraltar and the second did not, but it was the phrase in regard to Parliament that became the center of the dispute. The British insisted that the monarch could not circumvent Parliament and that the promise had been made in good faith but could not be kept because of public sentiment in favor of keeping Gibraltar and the refusal of Parliament to consider the issue. Spain maintained that the sole reason for including the phrase about Parliament was to provide the British with an excuse to retain Gibraltar and that the British had not only acted in bad faith but had deliberately misled Spain.[42]

The bitter two-year controversy was not resolved before war broke out in 1725, and Spain launched another attack on Gibraltar. This siege was less severe than the first, and commentators took more note of the high number of Spanish deserters and the tendency of the British cannons (78 out of 126) to explode than they did of the bombardment itself.[43] In the parliamentary debates that preceded the Treaty of Seville, signed in 1729, a majority in the House of Lords, having raised the issue of the letter promising to cede Gibraltar with the consent of Parliament, demanded that the king of Spain formally relinquish all claims to Gibraltar. The Spanish refused to issue a statement or to respond directly, but they remained silent rather than repeat their claim to the territory. An unofficial border was now established between the Iberian Peninsula and Gibraltar. The Spanish had established a fortified line beyond the range of the British guns and this was the official line of demarcation although unofficially there was a "neutral" zone between the British and Spanish lines.

It was not until the Seven Years' War broke out in 1756 that the issue of the return of Gibraltar was once again raised. The British admiral, Sir John Byng (George's son), did not effectively challenge the French fleet or reinforce Gibraltar or Port Mahon in Minorca. Consequently, the French took Port Mahon on June 28, and the furor this aroused in Britain led to the court-martial of Byng. It also led to a diplomatic initiative to procure Spain's entry into the war alongside Britain. In a letter to the Spanish minister at Madrid, in August 1757, William Pitt the Elder asked that the minister approach the king, because the king had been strongly advised to return Gibraltar to Spain if Spain entered the war against the French and secured the return of Port Mahon for Britain. Gibraltar was still considered more valuable as a negotiating chip than as a base by the government.

The British king and several leading ministers still believed that the limitations of Gibraltar reduced its value as a military base, whereas the Spanish determination to recover it would allow Britain to trade it for a far more valuable possession. The difficulty they faced was in convincing Parliament and the public, who held Gibraltar in far greater esteem, to accept this course of action. The fall of Port Mahon meant the population of Britain might accept the return of Gibraltar, but Spain did not respond to Pitt's overture. Spain was still considering the advantages and disadvantages of a new war, and the British suggestions were less than credible in light of the earlier letter by the king of Britain that had promised, with the consent of Parliament, to resolve this very issue.

Spain ultimately entered the war against Britain in 1762, fundamentally altering the conflict. The Treaty of Paris, signed in 1763, returned Minorca to Britain. As soon as the British confirmed the return of Minorca, they dropped the question of Gibraltar. In retrospect, this was Spain's best opportunity to recover "the Rock." The events that followed would soon eliminate any chance that Gibraltar would be returned to Spain under any terms.

When Britain was not in possession of Minorca, and so could not use it as a base from which to monitor and attack the French fleet at Toulon, Gibraltar demonstrated its value as the guardian of the Mediterranean. In addition, as the British extended their empire and British ships carried raw materials and refined textiles over long distances, Gibraltar took on new significance. If the wall surrounding the harbor was repaired and the docks repaired and expanded, Gibraltar could be used as a refueling and refitting station for British ships engaged in either trade or war.

There was still no official border, but just beyond the Spanish line of fortifications, the town of San Roque carried on the traditions of both Spain and Gibraltar, until Gibraltar's residents, who fled in 1704, could return. There were 2,710 inhabitants on "the Rock" in 1767, and according to the official register, 467 were British civilians, 1,460 were Catholics of non-British nationality (including some Spaniards and Genoese fishermen), and 783 were Jewish. The development of the town was linked to the British military garrison and the commercial opportunities it provided, and by 1756–1757, it was clear that Gibraltar was a British colony.[44] Many of the Genoese and Jews living there were traders or provided supplies to the garrison, and they depended on trade with the British military force—Gibraltar was primarily a military base, and the relatively small community supported itself by providing the basic needs of the military personnel. Gibraltar had also not developed into a trading or commercial center of any importance; the only significant European trade was the illegal smuggling of goods into Spain.

The War of American Independence, which began in April 1775 as a conflict between Britain and its 13 American colonies, expanded to encompass a struggle between the major European powers. By 1779, Britain appeared to be at the very low ebb of the tide. The British were fighting the colonists over a great distance and were at war with the French, who were delivering supplies and reinforcements to North America. The French, embittered by previous conflicts and the treaty that ended the Seven Years' War, assisted the colonists and ultimately declared war against Britain. In 1759, King Charles III of Spain had inherited the Crown, and with it the desire to regain Gibraltar. France and Spain signed a secret agreement in April 1779 stipulating that Spain would enter the war against Britain, and France would fight until Spain recovered Gibraltar. For Spain, it seemed the perfect opportunity to inflict a humiliating defeat on the British and at the same time to restore the territorial integrity of Spain by regaining Gibraltar.[45]

Spanish forces attacked Gibraltar from June 1779 until February of 1783, and the unofficial border that was established ceased to exist, as Spanish soldiers occupied the "neutral ground." During this period, the garrison was either blockaded by land and sea, or came under systematic bombardment. There were massive preparations and an additional heavy bombardment, meant to precede a direct attack. The direct attack was never carried out because the British conducted a midnight raid to destroy the advance Spanish lines. Spain also carried out an assault by "floating batteries" (gun platforms with sides and a roof of reinforced wood with a layer of damp cloth in between to prevent the platforms from catching fire) that were effectively countered by the use of "hot" shots or projectiles that were heated before being fired by cannons at the attacking fleet.

Although the Spanish bombardment produced significant casualties, it was the blockade and lack of supplies and fresh fruit or vegetables that weakened the British garrison to the extent that victory seemed within reach of Spain. The garrison was nearly starved into submission, and the British were only able to resupply on a few occasions by sending an entire naval squadron to fight off the enemy ships enforcing the blockade. Furthermore, the weakened condition of individuals, combined with a diet devoid of fruit and vegetables, caused hundreds of deaths from disease and epidemic.[46]

While Sir George Eliott, the governor of Gibraltar, was undertaking the necessary preparations to withstand the siege, British diplomats made a proposal offering Gibraltar in exchange for Spain's withdrawal from the American War of Independence. It was the commander of the British fleet in Lisbon, Commodore Johnson, who made the offer in 1779. Spain took this initiative more seriously than previous overtures, in part because the offer was conditional upon the acquisition of Puerto Rico and Port Oran (in present-day Algeria) by Britain and the payment for all materials Britain had used in improving the fortifications. Nevertheless, the offer and subsequent discussions produced no results.

The last attempt at negotiation on the question of Gibraltar and peace with Spain occurred in December 1782. It was Spain that proposed that Britain could retain Minorca but give up West Florida. Gibraltar would be restored to Spain on the condition that France found an equivalent territory to turn over to the British. This was the only proposal for the cession of Gibraltar that was ever approved by the British cabinet. Before the king could even bring the matter before Parliament, however, the situation was altered by the news that negotiations for peace had begun between Britain and the American colonists.

Sir George Eliott, depicted here by renowned English portrait painter Sir Joshua Reynolds, served as governor of Gibraltar from 1777 to 1783. In 1779, during the War of American Independence, a combined French and Spanish force attempted to seize Gibraltar from the British. Despite facing 100,000 troops and 48 ships in September 1782, the British were able to hold out and the siege ended the following year.

When the king mentioned Gibraltar to Parliament two days later, that body was not favorably inclined toward any agreement that would give away a territory retained at a very high cost during a war in which Britain had few glorious moments. The

British countered Spain's proposal with an offer to give Florida to Spain, and under the terms of the Treaty of Versailles, signed on September 3, 1783, Britain retained Gibraltar.

The town and the garrison of Gibraltar had endured the Great Siege, which had reduced the total population. Some had died of starvation, some had been killed by shells, and some had left Gibraltar on the ships that brought reinforcements and supplies, never to return. The siege strengthened the ties between Gibraltar's inhabitants and Great Britain and hardened the resolve of the peninsula's residents. It also hardened the resolve of the British politicians and public against the return of Gibraltar to Spain.[47] Perhaps the most significant aspect of the Great Siege was that it "so increased the pride and interest of the English in their possession that, it made an end, once and for all . . . of all possibility of its ever being surrendered, short of a national collapse."[48]

Spain might not have reconciled itself to the loss of Gibraltar, but the British seemed to have finally accepted their possession of it. Britain made no more serious attempts to trade Gibraltar; the country was fully aware of the national view and esteem in which the territory was held. After the Great Siege, when the British demonstrated their ability to defend and secure "the Rock" during a major assault, Gibraltar experienced an increase in settlement, as well as the return of merchants and other traders. In addition to being a symbol of British endurance in the wake of the devastating loss of the American colonies, Gibraltar also gained a more practical significance. When Europe was preoccupied, at first by the French Revolution and the subsequent French Revolutionary Wars, and later by the Napoleonic Wars, Gibraltar served as a naval base rather than simply an impregnable land fortress.

Gibraltar was in the right location to serve as a port for British ships headed to Egypt, and foreign ships sailing into and out of the Mediterranean could be monitored or interrupted by a naval force operating from Gibraltar. It was only after the outbreak of the French Revolution, however, that the true value of Gibraltar became apparent. Anglo-Spanish relations during the period of the French Revolutionary Wars were curious. Old resentments lingered, but in the wake of the overthrow of the monarchy in France and the spread of revolutionary ideas and violence, Britain and Spain formed an alliance. In 1793, France declared itself to be at war with Britain and the Netherlands and, after a brief four-week interval, went to war with Spain, as well.

France defeated Spain, resulting in a peace agreement signed in July 1795, and the more conservative Directory came to power in France after the fall of Robespierre and the Committee of Public Safety, who had initiated the Reign of Terror. As a result of these two events, Spain abruptly altered its foreign policy and signed the Treaty of Aranjuez with France in June 1796. The secret clause of that treaty, which said Spain would return Louisiana to France after Spain and France had conquered Gibraltar, demonstrated that Spain had not reconciled itself to the loss of Gibraltar. Britain, facing an Anglo-Spanish alliance at the same time as mutinies by British sailors, was forced to evacuate units from the Mediterranean, which was often referred to between roughly 1793 and 1795 as a "French lake."[49]

Gibraltar was of supreme importance during a period in British history when the empire had no presence or possession in the Mediterranean. However, this importance did not stem from the ability to control the passage of ships through the Strait of Gibraltar; the nature and strength of the current and the winds in the passage made it difficult for ships in the Gibraltar harbor to emerge and intercept enemy fleets passing in or out of the Mediterranean. Rather, Gibraltar was an ideal central location from which to gather, organize, and pass along intelligence.

Gibraltar had its flaws: It still did not have docking facilities that were in any way adequate for the maintenance of a naval force. Nevertheless, as British Admiral Lord Nelson indicated, it was the only place he could obtain a mast. In other words, Gibraltar was the only outlying British base at which ships could refit and obtain supplies, and the British Navy appreciated the respite that Gibraltar offered, despite its inadequacies. Gibraltar was valuable as a naval base that could not easily be taken by land or sea and as a point from which the enemy could be monitored.

Eventually, the British Navy increased its success and was able to regain control over the seas. The fleet sailed back into the Mediterranean, where it conquered Minorca in December 1798 and Malta in 1800. These conquests did not diminish the value of Gibraltar, and, in fact, in 1800, Admiral Lord St. Vincent went to live in Gibraltar. "[H]e [Lord St. Vincent] was centrally placed to receive information, to give orders, and especially to hasten by his unflagging personal supervision the work of supply and repair upon which the efficiency of a fleet primarily depends."[50]

The island of Malta, near Sicily, would ultimately prove to have more advantages than Gibraltar, but Gibraltar played a key role in the British struggles between 1800 and 1815. Lord Nelson used Gibraltar as a base from which to pursue the Franco-Spanish forces after Spain joined with Napoleon and declared war on Britain in 1804. Immediately after the Battle of Trafalgar, at which Nelson decisively defeated the French and Spanish fleets, the British fleet entered Gibraltar to undertake necessary repairs before carrying out burials. Following the British victory at Trafalgar, Napoleon established the Continental System, an embargo against British goods, and decreed that any vessel stopping at a British port and proceeding to one on the continent would be confiscated.

Gibraltar was now one of the few places from which goods could be conveyed to Europe without risking the confiscation of valuable merchant vessels. It was a well-known fact that at least one-third of the "merchants" in Gibraltar smuggled goods into Spain, a situation that had been a virtually constant source of tension between Britain and Spain. Smuggling on "the Rock," at times openly tolerated and at other times discouraged or prosecuted by the British government, now became a matter of vital national interest and was officially organized and coordinated. After Napoleon occupied Spain, the Spanish were supplied by the smugglers on Gibraltar and encouraged their activities.

The more of Europe that Napoleon annexed, the greater was Gibraltar's prosperity. This was also reflected in the meteoric rise of its population from 3,000 in 1804 to 10,000 in 1814. Not all of Gibraltar's income was based on illegal activities, but the few businesses that were established, including bakeries, a cannery, and a brewery, had difficulty in sustaining themselves and often only operated for brief periods. Smugglers continued to make a great profit, and in 1814 two individuals were listed as smugglers on the census report.[51] In 1815, when Napoleon's conquests ended, Gibraltar's prosperity immediately receded into the doldrums of a severe depression, but by then, Gibraltar had served Britain and itself well.[52]

The 1815 Congress of Vienna decided the political fate of Europe. It provided peace to a war-weary continent and also a permanent peace between Spain and Britain that has endured to the present day. The grievances—Gibraltar and colonial rivalry—that repeatedly pushed the countries into war in the eighteenth century remained, but "the old standing hostility had come to an end: Spain was minor both as a nuisance and as an opportunity."[53]

Spain had been eclipsed as a great power by Britain, and although the period of direct conflict and assaults against Gibraltar ended, the dispute over territorial jurisdiction and rightful ownership of Gibraltar did not. In 1830, as a result of its contribution to the British war effort, Gibraltar was made a Crown colony, recognized as a community separate from the military garrison, and its citizens were officially granted specific civil rights. The civilians also gained some control over their own affairs; however, the authority of the royal governor remained nearly absolute, except when Gibraltarians successfully appealed to the British government to override the governor's decisions.

In the decades following the Congress of Vienna, Spain attempted to develop its own industries and reverted to its policy of preventing smuggling across the Spanish-Gibraltar border. Spain's efforts were not successful, and smuggling continued to flourish. This illicit trade was so prominent by 1856 that the governor of Gibraltar, Sir Robert Gardiner, attempted to take action by complaining to British officials. The merchants and citizens of Gibraltar, however, protested the governor's actions suppressing their activities, and the British government, which had a vested interest in commercial ventures, decided that smuggling was Spain's problem and recalled the governor. The issue of smuggling led to the resurrection of the territorial dispute, although in this case the emphasis was on British jurisdiction in the bay or waters surrounding Gibraltar.

As in the case of the land adjacent to the fortress that was given to Britain by the Treaty of Utrecht, no specific boundary in the waters had been included. The British, using the same range-of-guns argument they had applied to the land boundaries, claimed a jurisdiction of approximately 3 miles (4.8 kilometers), whereas the Spanish wanted the bay divided in half. Britain protested that, at times, its vessels were seized by the Spanish or that they were not allowed to aid their own ships coming toward the shore within sight of the fortress and sometimes within range of Gibraltar's guns. Both sides fired on each other's ships in the bay, and the dispute could not be resolved by negotiation. The effective range of the guns of both sides continued to have a considerable impact on the territory both on land and at sea that each side could claim and over which it could exert control. Despite territorial arguments, a number of changes had occurred on Gibraltar, and by the end of the nineteenth century, it had the appearance of a real community rather than just a military garrison and encampment. The population had ceased to be an arbitrary collection of transients, and a number of individuals who lived on Gibraltar had been born there. Still, its status as a disputed territory was no closer to being resolved.

4

Border Disputes
& Conflict
in Europe

There was a profound change in the status and nature of Gibraltar between the mid-eighteenth century and the early nineteenth century. The best description of the difference between Gibraltar before and after the Napoleonic Wars is provided by Sir William G. F. Jackson in his history of Gibraltar. According to Jackson,

> For Gibraltar [the end of the Napoleonic Wars] marked the watershed between the first two centuries of British sovereignty. In the first hundred years Gibraltar had lived at war; in the second, the Rock was to enjoy unbroken peace and modest prosperity. Two things gave Gibraltar her century of peace: the *Pax Britannica* of the Victorian era, and the debilitating effects of political instability upon the Spanish realm. A further Spanish military attack on Gibraltar became unthinkable and, although the Spanish claim to sovereignty was never forgotten, peaceful coexistence was allowed to develop.[54]

The community might have stabilized and enjoyed increasing prosperity, but the debate over political and territorial jurisdiction escalated, and the border between Gibraltar and Spain remained arbitrary. Because there was no enclosed harbor, the cession of the harbor to Britain by treaty did not have an exact or literal meaning. The British claimed a 3-mile (4.8-kilometer) radius based on the distance their guns could fire, but Spain insisted that, aside from the fortress, no territory on land or at sea had been ceded. As most of the bay fell within the range of Spanish cannons, and Spain claimed the beaches and land in front of the fort, problems were likely to occur.

During the nineteenth century, as the official dispute continued with virtually no changes in the British or Spanish positions, Gibraltar was transformed from a military garrison and a town entirely dependent upon it into something quite different. Unlike in the eighteenth century, when the civilian population had never been larger than that of the garrison (which fluctuated between 3,000 and 5,500), by 1813, the civilian community was more than twice the size of the military garrison. This caused overcrowding and the further deterioration of sanitary conditions.

The makeup of the community also changed. In the previous century, the population of Gibraltar consisted mainly of Genoese and Jewish settlers, with a relatively small number of British, Spanish, Portuguese, or other nationalities. In the nineteenth century, the number of Jews and Italians did not increase by a significant amount, and although there were immigrants from other countries (including Austria, Denmark, the German territories, Switzerland, the United States, Sicily, and Greece), they represented only a fraction of Gibraltar's population.[55] The sizable population increase, then, was attributable to an influx of Portuguese immigrants and an increase in the number of Spanish, who traveled across the permeable border between Spain and Gibraltar.

It is impossible to determine the exact number of Spanish immigrants or the extent to which they exerted an influence on the culture of Gibraltarians. H. W. Howes, in a 1951 work that focuses on identifying and tracing the development of the people of Gibraltar, argues that there has been a tendency to overemphasize the Spanish presence and effect on the population. Howes claims that, because many of the Spanish immigrants were women, it was wrongly assumed that they would exert a considerable influence over the culture. Anja Kellerman, in her work on language politics and identity in Gibraltar, criticizes Howes's approach, because he only counts men above the age of 17. She objects strongly to omitting women from the statistics and implies that, whether by intent or accident, Howes is also eliminating women from history by failing to acknowledge their presence. Kellerman's key point, however, is in regard to the conclusions that Howes draws from his figures:

> According to his [Howes's] figures for 1814, the Spanish
> would amount to a mere 16.5% (31% Genoese and Italians,

20% Portuguese, 15% Jews, 12.5% British, and 4% Minorcans). The list amounts to a total of 3,197, all of which are men. Yet the civilian population was 10,136 *ergo* HOWES' nationality count left 6,939 persons, i.e. 68% of the population, unaccounted for. From what is known about the Gibraltarian marriage pattern, the better part of these 68% of women and children were either Spanish or born to Spanish mothers. . . . HOWES plainly calculates away a crucial linguistic and cultural element [emphasis and bold type in the original][56]

The influence of the Spanish on the developing community of Gibraltar is far more difficult to assess than the numbers or other aspects of its population. There is no doubt, however, that the Spanish influence was much stronger during and after the Napoleonic era, as a result of the permeable nature of the border in this period, than in the previous century, when Anglo-Spanish relations and conflicts made the border a true, if arbitrary, dividing line.

Along with the changing demographics of the community, its relationship to the garrison also changed. As a result of the increased prosperity and the willingness of individuals to settle permanently in Gibraltar, the civilian community began to carry out functions and developed an identity separate from the military garrison. Prosperity and increased opportunity also created a myriad of problems, including overcrowding, lack of sanitation, and inadequate social services. These problems were exacerbated by the continued growth of the population throughout the nineteenth century.

British officials took steps to limit population growth and address social issues in the late nineteenth century, but first they had to deal with problems caused by the absence of an official border. In 1826, when a British ship was wrecked and washed up on the neutral territory between mainland Spain and the fortress of Gibraltar, Spanish forces at sea prevented the British from rendering assistance. The British were outraged and protested that, in

times of peace, the preservation of human life should take precedence over abstract matters such as territory or jurisdiction. The
debate over jurisdiction in this instance had little to do with political or diplomatic interests. The loss of life in this incident had
demonstrated the dire consequences of the failure to establish an
official border under the Treaty of Utrecht. The British foreign
secretary, George Canning, sent an official letter to the Spanish
minister in Madrid, Conde de Alcudia, noting the following:[57]

> In the absence of all mention by the Treaty of Utrecht of any
> boundary, real or imaginary, of the Port of Gibraltar . . . it
> becomes necessary in the first place to look for a natural
> boundary in the trending of the Coast. That boundary is to be
> found in the curvature of the Coast terminating in the Punta
> Mala, the whole of which space is within the range of the guns
> been considered as the limit of the Port to the northward; and
> from the time of the Fortress coming into the possession of
> Great Britain, Port Charges have . . . invariably been levied on
> all vessels anchoring within that limit.[58]

Canning mentions the now familiar British argument in
regard to jurisdiction over all territory covered by British cannons, but he also refers to long-standing practice. Since the
treaty set no specific boundary at sea, there are no territorial
waters expressly denied to the British. Canning thus supports
the British claim by noting that de facto rights had been established by the actual practice of landing and anchoring ships in
the waters adjacent to the "neutral territory." Canning's letter
provoked a Spanish response and the issue of jurisdiction continued to plague relations between the two nations. Spain was
extremely sensitive, not out of fear of British attack, but because
of its claim that Gibraltar was part of Spain. Spain also resented
and lodged constant complaints about smuggling, which continued because it was profitable and because the British were
strong enough to exercise de facto control over the land and
water around the fortress.

George Canning, depicted in this 1826 sketch, served as British foreign secretary from 1807 to 1809 and again from 1822 to 1827. Canning was instrumental in attempting to establish an official border around Gibraltar after the Spanish failed to render help to a British ship when it washed ashore in neutral territory between mainland Spain and the fortress of Gibraltar in 1826.

In 1858, Spain proposed settling the issue of the boundary on land as a way to reduce tensions between their country and Britain. Spain still claimed Gibraltar was Spanish territory and did not relinquish territorial claims to the waters in the bay, which were described as washing up on land that clearly belonged to Spain. It also claimed all land designated as neutral ground, stating that the Treaty of Utrecht only gave the fortress to Britain and not a single inch of territory beyond it. The Spanish minister, however, suggested that his country might be willing to concede jurisdiction of the territory on land as far as the cannons could fire, while asserting that there was no question on jurisdiction at sea since the country whose coasts are washed by the waters has absolute jurisdiction.[59]

Spain proposed that the matter be resolved by a committee of two English and two Spanish representatives, who would be confined to using the Treaty of Utrecht as a basis or guide to determine the land boundaries that had caused so many difficulties. In essence, Spain was willing to officially designate the land between Gibraltar and the Spanish lines as neutral territory in exchange for formal British recognition of Spain's claim to all waters in the bay.[60]

The British refused to engage in a discussion about the Spanish initiative, which was hardly surprising. Spain was attempting to gain formal British recognition for its operations in the bay but was refusing to discuss other issues, such as formal recognition of Gibraltar as British territory. Furthermore, Spanish recognition of the neutral territory on land had little appeal, because Britain could ensure that it remained neutral simply by maintaining the cannons that covered that stretch of land. There was no real need to address the issue of the "neutral territory," as the British occupied part of it and the Spanish had built a line of defenses there in 1730 that enabled them to cut off all contact between Gibraltar and mainland Spain whenever they so desired.

Officially, the dispute continued, but unofficially British and Spanish authorities had worked out an informal system with regard to territorial waters. The line of demarcation remained fairly stable during this period, and in that sense the border was less arbitrary than in previous decades, when the land occupied by British and Spanish forces had shifted several times. It was extremely arbitrary, however, in the sense that there was a remarkable difference between official statements by both countries and the practical arrangements carried out by British and Spanish authorities responsible for Gibraltar and the adjacent territory under Spanish control. British ships continued to anchor off the beaches, where British and Spanish sentries came within 350 yards of one another at the closest point, and British harbor authorities exercised control over ships landing on the beaches, as well as those moored at the dockyard some distance away and out of range of Spanish cannons.

The British were not convinced that the threat to Gibraltar had entirely dissipated and carried out further work on the fortifications and the naval dockyard. The old cannons, which were loaded from the front and were inaccurate beyond a 3-mile (4.8-kilometer) radius, were replaced. The new cannons were loaded from the back and had grooves in the barrel, which made them more accurate and increased their range to 5 miles (8 kilometers). A debate over the improvements to the fortifications of Gibraltar broke out in the British Parliament, where opponents said they were too costly and their effect was likely to be nullified if there was a war.

The Spanish also had new cannons that covered the entire bay, as well as the fortress, with their 5-mile (8-kilometer) range. The opposition in Parliament failed to reverse the decision to improve the fortress, so Gibraltar changed considerably between 1826 and 1853. During this period, the British reinforced the fortress walls, placed cannons in every position from which they could be effectively fired, and built a seawall or mole, that protected ships anchoring on the western end of "the Rock." In 1846, the harbor was improved by extending the seawall and building fortified positions to defend it. Not all of the changes were for the better. Because of a severe shortage of labor, British authorities resorted to sending convicts to Gibraltar, where they were forced to do the heavy labor involved in building the seawall and improving the defenses.

During the period between 1826 and 1853, the British reinforced Gibraltar's walls, placed cannons in every available location, and built a seawall to protect ships that anchored on the western side of the peninsula. Pictured here are British soldiers standing guard on a bluff above the rocky cliffs of Gibraltar in 1862.

This practice sent a number of unsavory individuals to Gibraltar, and foreign visitors commented unfavorably on the nature of the population. The Marquis de Custine, a French aristocrat and travel writer known for his description of Russia, minced no words in writing about the residents of Gibraltar in the mid-nineteenth century: "The dregs of the Mediterranean make up the population of Gibraltar . . . riff-raff no state no family would acknowledge theirs, a gathering of bandits . . . in consort with highwaymen and pirates."[61] Convicts and dregs of the Mediterranean were not the only inhabitants on "the Rock," however, and overall, both the garrison soldiers and the civilians were more respectable than in previous centuries. The community was a blending of various ethnic groups, consisting of smugglers, convicts, soldiers, respectable merchants, and the families of British soldiers.

One of the bitterest issues between Spain and Britain was the British toleration of illegal trade and the unsavory individuals known to be smuggling goods into Spain. After the seizure of Gibraltar, the military garrison had to be supplied, and Britain was forced to tolerate known smugglers, because few other merchants were willing to reside on "the Rock." By the nineteenth century, however, the situation had changed, and there were a significant number of Gibraltar residents who did not engage in smuggling. Smuggling remained profitable, though, and smugglers continued to be tolerated and even unofficially supported by the government in Britain.

When Spain argued that Gibraltar should be returned, because the British violated the clause prohibiting smuggling, it might have exaggerated the extent of the illegal trade. Accounts by foreign visitors to Gibraltar in the nineteenth century, however, lend credence to the Spanish position. The description of the smugglers on Gibraltar provided in 1840 by Charles Dembowski, a Franco-Polish baron, suggests that the Spanish protests were justified:

> Those red coats which in London were to me a source of joy here fill me with the same sorrow which Spaniards must feel . . . You should see the shamelessness of the Andalucian smugglers, spoon-fed and almost respected by the authorities. They strut about the streets of Gibraltar as if they owned the place. Woe to the Spanish customs officer who forgets

Gibraltar is not Spanish and dares enter the neutral zone or British waters in the heat of the chase.[62]

The British authorities on Gibraltar often looked the other way, which encouraged the smuggling of goods. Spain was most embittered not by the smuggling itself but by Britain's response to Spanish protests. The British minster of state, Lord Palmerston, sent a note to the Spanish government stating that each country has a right to enforce its own laws, but that laws attempting to prevent free commercial trade are antiquated. He suggested that Spain can resolve the issue of smuggling by revising its own tariff to allow for increased trade. The Spanish government could hardly be expected to react well to the suggestion that the solution was to lower tariffs and allow British goods to flood Spain.

It is ironic that the governor of Gibraltar at the time, Sir Robert Gardiner, was sympathetic to the Spanish objection to smuggling and was concerned by the detrimental effect the smuggling trade had on the men under his command. Gardiner pointed out that soldiers were likely to be approached and bribed while on sentry duty and argued that soldiers accepting bribes to abandon their duties had a demoralizing effect on the garrison.[63]

Gardiner's attempt to act against the merchants carrying on illegal trade brought him into conflict with the British government, to whom the merchants of Gibraltar had sent a direct appeal. The government once again put its commercial interests over diplomacy or Anglo-Spanish relations. Gardiner was recalled, and the British view can be reduced to a single sentence uttered by the officials who sided with the merchants: "Smuggling is Spain's problem, not Britain's."[64] This attitude would have made it extremely difficult to improve Anglo-Spanish relations under any circumstances, and it added a further dimension to the border dispute.

The British insisted that they had the right to territory they occupied outside the fortress and protested bitterly when the

Spanish refused to allow them to assist a British ship in distress in Spanish waters. On the other hand, they refused to allow Spain to operate in the neutral zone to prevent smuggling or to arrest individuals who were circumventing the Spanish authorities. This British double standard and its refusal to make any significant concessions infuriated Spain and ensured that the border would remain arbitrary. This rigid policy and unwillingness to assist Spain in preventing illegal activities further motivated Spain to recover Gibraltar by any means possible.

At the same time that British efforts were transforming Gibraltar into a fortified base, and Anglo-Spanish relations were deteriorating, external events were occurring that would have just as great an impact on "the Rock." The invention of the steam engine and the use of steam to power ships were first applied around 1788 and took on increased significance when the first successful commercial venture was established by Robert Fulton in 1807. The advent of steam vessels had more of an impact on Gibraltar and on traffic in the Mediterranean Sea than in other areas. The Mediterranean had long periods without any wind, and the winds were often erratic. The unreliability of the winds meant that oars were still used to power ships in the Mediterranean well into the nineteenth century, whereas sailing vessels were used in nearly every other body of water. So the ability to send steam-powered ships quickly through the Mediterranean at all times of the year increased trade. Gibraltar, situated as it was at the entrance to the Mediterranean, became more important, as well.[65]

The Crimean War of the 1850s was fought, with few exceptions, by sailing vessels, but it became apparent that any nation that could control the sea would be able to quickly transport troops and supplies across vast distances. Although the Great Siege had solidified the romanticized view of Gibraltar among the British public, the debate about its usefulness continued in Parliament. Some members argued that Gibraltar was too vulnerable to a siege by Spain to be a viable base; others countered with Spain's suggestion that Britain did not have a rightful claim to the territory. One member of Parliament, John Bright, said "England took possession of the Rock when she was not expressly at war with Spain, and she retains it against all moral codes."[66]

The Spanish essayist and novelist Angel Ganivet, writing in the nineteenth century, assessed the situation accurately when he wrote: "Gibraltar is a force for England so long as Spain is weak; but if Spain were strong it would become a vulnerable point and would lose its raison d'etre."[67] This statement has broader implications than the obvious suggestion that a powerful Spain could besiege Gibraltar and force the British to supply it by sea. Gibraltar's lack of resources and its geographic position make its border with the Iberian Peninsula more artificial than boundaries in other conquered territories or colonies. Independence is not a viable option for Gibraltar, and it only had a sizable population after the British established a military garrison there and trade with Europe increased.

Although the argument that only Spain can exercise sovereignty over the territory is disputable, it is true that Gibraltar's viability as a military and naval base ceases to be a question if it comes under Spanish control. Gibraltar is connected to Spain by a narrow isthmus and the Spanish have the option of supplying it by land or sea. Spain had so completely neglected the defenses of Gibraltar that Sir George Rooke was able to seize it in 1704, but this does not alter the fact that it was easier for Spain than for Britain to occupy and defend it. The British had to maintain the fortress by sheer power of their naval force during periods when it was besieged or when Spain closed off the border. Thus, if one considers Gibraltar solely in political and geographic terms, the border seems extremely artificial, and British occupation of "the Rock" is a clear symbol of Spain's weaknesses, as Ganivet points out.

Between 1890 and 1904, Spain fought and lost a war with the United States. One event of the Spanish-American War is of great significance to the dispute over Gibraltar. After the United States declared war on Spain in 1898, Spain began to construct emplacements around the Bay of Algeciras and ordered new long-range guns from the German arms manufacturer Krupps. Britain viewed the guns as a direct threat to Gibraltar, and demanded that Spain halt all work. The British government, with Lord Salisbury as prime minister and Lord Landsdowne as foreign minister, proposed an agreement under which the needs of Spain would clearly be subordinated to those of Britain. The key provisions of this proposal are as follows:

THE SPANISH-AMERICAN WAR

By the 1890s, all that remained of the once great Spanish empire in the Americas were Cuba and Puerto Rico. In 1895, native Cubans resented Spanish policies, especially increased taxes on sugar, and a revolt broke out. Spain resorted to increasingly brutal measures under General Valeriano Weyler to defeat the rebels. Weyler established camps and moved most of the population into them where they died by the thousands as a result of overcrowding and unsanitary conditions. Newspapers in the United States, such as Joseph Pulitzer's *New York World*, published sensationalized stories about Spanish atrocities. The United States had initially refused to become involved and remained neutral, but President William McKinley, who came into office in March 1897, began to criticize Spain's inhumane treatment of Cubans. General Weyler was recalled by Spain late in 1897, but riots by army officers in Havana suggested that Madrid might not be able to control the situation.

McKinley ordered the U.S. battleship, the *Maine*, to Havana, to remind Spain of the presence and views of the United States and to be available for evacuations if necessary. The publication of a private letter stolen from Enrique Dupuy de Lome, the Spanish ambassador in Washington D.C., which ridiculed McKinley, and the explosion of the battleship *Maine* on February 15, which killed 266 sailors, resulted in the outbreak of war between the United States and Spain. A weak and declining Spain was no match for the United States, which had become a major industrial power and increased the size and strength of its navy in the decades preceding the war.

Article II, that Spain not take the side of Britain's enemies; Article III, that Spain undertake the defense of Gibraltar from land and not mount guns within gunshot of Gibraltar; Article IV, that in time of war the Spanish government allow the British government to enlist Spaniards in the British Army; and an additional note, Britain reserved the right to invade Spain if in the British view the invasion of Spain by a third power threatened Gibraltar.[68]

The war lasted just over three months. Commodore George Dewey crushed the Spanish fleet in Manila Bay and U.S. armed forces defeated the Spanish in Cuba. Spain and the United States met in Paris in October 1898 to discuss peace terms. The Spanish representative was willing to recognize the independence of Cuba as well as to cede Puerto Rico and Guam to the United States. The United States demand that Spain also cede the Philippines, softened by the offer of a $20 million payment, was initially refused by Spain but in the end it had little choice. The Treaty of Paris, which included all of the provisions discussed above, was signed on December 10, 1898. The treaty exemplified the declining power of Spain and the rise of a new and powerful United States that would officially enter the European diplomatic circle as a result of the Spanish-American War. The loss of possessions, as well as prestige, because of the war with the United States increased Spain's resolve to restore its own territorial integrity. The final conquest of Gibraltar in 1462 and the expulsion of the Jews and Moors in 1492 had represented the peak of Spain's power. But Spain's inability to end the British occupation, or to even procure an official line of demarcation, was a constant reminder of its weaknesses. Despite the vulnerability of Gibraltar and its lack of natural resources, the British occupied the ground in front of the fortress and resupplied Gibraltar by sea at will. The truth was more complex and the vulnerability of Gibraltar caused several leading British statesmen to have grave concerns over its retention. In Spain, pride and nationalism shaped perception and national leaders could always arouse support by vowing to restore "the Rock."

This proposal was entirely unrealistic and further infuriated the Spanish government. Essentially, the British would give Spain permission to mount guns in territory Spain already possessed, if Spain guaranteed it would not go to war against Britain and allowed Britain to send troops into Spain, if necessary, to defend Gibraltar. Spain was at its lowest point, but the rapid conclusion of the war, which demonstrated Spain's weaknesses and America's strengths, allowed Spain to inform the British in March 1899 that no further expansion of the defenses of Algeciras were necessary. If the British persisted with their demands, Spain threatened to place the matter before the international community, and Britain, aware that few if any countries would support its position, dropped the matter. The continuing decline of Spanish power, combined with British arrogance and expansion, led to inevitable conflict and bitter feelings at the highest levels of government and disagreements between diplomats.

Historians assessing the causes of World War I see the period between the 1880s and the outbreak of the war in 1914 as crucial. They deemed the war had three major causes: (1) the division of Europe into two opposing alliances; (2) the growth of armies and military staffs that influenced national policy; and (3) increased rivalry and competition for colonies and markets. The crisis that broke out after the assassination of the Austrian Archduke Franz Ferdinand in Sarajevo on June 28, 1914, could not (for various reasons beyond the scope of our discussion) be resolved by diplomacy, and, instead, a war engulfed most European nations. The Central Powers (Austria-Hungary, Germany, and the Ottoman Empire) fought against the Allied Powers (Britain, France, Russia, Italy—which entered the war only in 1915—and ultimately the United States).

Gibraltar had a role, but not a key one, in the Great War, which lasted from 1914 to 1918. Gibraltar was entirely vulnerable if Spain joined the war, and thus, Britain had to be extremely cautious about using it as a port until it was determined that Spain would not join the war against Britain and France. Also, the use of submarines by the Germans meant that Gibraltar

On June 28, 1914, Gavrilo Princip, a Serbian who supported independence for the Southern Slavic people, assassinated Archduke Franz Ferdinand (pictured here with his wife, Sophie, minutes before the assassination) in Sarajevo. The event triggered the start of World War I, during which Gibraltar served as a key base for the Allied forces (Britain, France, Russia, and the United States), which were opposed by the Central Powers (Germany, Austria-Hungary, and the Ottoman Empire).

could no longer even monitor the movement of enemy fleets, let alone intercept them. It had always been difficult to intercept ships because of the current and winds, but now it was impossible even to monitor their entry and exit from the Mediterranean.

Britain's inability to track the movements of submarines is demonstrated by the collapse of Austria-Hungary in 1918. Fifteen U-Boats were still in the Mediterranean when Austria-Hungary collapsed and deprived them of bases in the Adriatic. The U-boats were ordered back to Germany at the end of October 1918, and 13 of them slipped past a blockade of British, American, Italian, Portuguese, and Brazilian warships positioned at the entry to the Strait of Gibraltar. Not only did the Allies not detect the submarines as they passed, but one U-boat fired its torpedoes and sank the British battleship *Britannia*, which was located at Cape Trafalgar.[69]

This incident shows the limitations of Gibraltar, but since Spain did not join the war, Gibraltar was utilized by the Allies. At least 80 merchant vessels that had been damaged by German submarines were repaired, and 350 Allied warships were supplied and overhauled at "the Rock." In April 1917, Gibraltar became the point from which convoys across the Atlantic and through the Mediterranean were organized. In general, the convoy system reduced the Allied shipping losses considerably, but it did not help in the Mediterranean, where the U-boats were extremely effective. About 5 of the estimated 13 million tons of Allied shipping lost during the war was sunk in the Mediterranean. The expanded port and docking facilities proved their worth, however, and Gibraltar prevented the loss of damaged ships by serving as a repair station. Gibraltar also allowed ships to refuel and acquire supplies without sailing all the way back to Britain. Gibraltar's worth, however, was increasingly dependent upon the neutrality of Spain.[70]

During the war, Spain was less than neutral in its actions, openly tolerating individuals who repaired and resupplied German submarines, but there was little the Allies could do because Gibraltar was so vulnerable. The area did not have enough drinkable water to meet the needs of its population, and thus the Allies depended on Spain to allow water to be provided by Algeciras and Ceuta. After the United States began to use Gibraltar as a base in 1917, the water shortage became critical, and the British government made an official request that was granted after a three-month delay, on the condition that water could not be loaded at Algeciras during the day.

The Germans could use the entire history of Gibraltar since 1704 to condemn the British and to persuade Spain to take its side in the war effort, and the British had no response acceptable to any Spaniard. Spain had not fared well in recent conflicts, though, and had colonial possessions as well as its own territorial integrity to lose if it entered the war on the losing side. Therefore, for the duration of the Great War, Spain remained a neutral nation, and continued to demand the return of Gibraltar but did not take any hostile action to do so, a fact that benefited Spain in the long term, because Britain and her allies won the war.[71]

Because the British relied on force to secure the area around the fortress when diplomacy failed, the absence of an official border on land or at sea increased the vulnerability of Gibraltar during wartime. The introduction of long-range artillery made the British increasingly uneasy, because it would be difficult to make Gibraltar completely secure if it was attacked by Spain or a coalition force that had secured Spain's assistance or neutrality. The presence of a civilian population that, since 1834, was in excess of 14,000, meant that it would be more difficult to procure the necessary supplies or to arrange the evacuation of civilians if Spain were to institute a siege and naval blockade. Unofficially, a border along the lines that the British and Spanish forces occupied was well established, although there was still no official border designation, and the dispute continued. The population growth, hazards posed by the advent of modern warfare and weaponry, as well as the difficulty in maintaining friendly relations between Britain and Spain caused serious problems. There is no question, however, that the border was less arbitrary between 1830 and 1920 than it was before or afterward. The border remained open during most of this period, there were no blockades or sieges, trade with Spain increased, the population remained fairly stable, and the number of individuals born on Gibraltar increased.

5

Hitler,
World War II,
and Gibraltar

The event that ultimately had the greatest impact on Gibraltar, and revealed that, despite appearances, the border was still arbitrary, was the rise to power of General Francisco Franco in 1939. The British were preoccupied with the military threat posed by Franco's authoritarian and nationalistic regime, which demanded the return of Gibraltar. Even more disconcerting was the connection between Franco and the Fascist nations of Italy and Germany, against whom Britain went to war in 1939. The German führer, Adolf Hitler, advocated the seizure of "the Rock" and created Operation Felix, in essence, a plan for a military assault on Gibraltar as part of an effort to sever British naval operations in the Mediterranean.

A successful conquest of Gibraltar, however, depended on either active assistance from Franco's Spain or, at the very least, permission for German troops to march through Spain. The British recognized the weaknesses of Gibraltar and prepared for the worst, evacuating 14,000 civilians. The British also built an airstrip on "neutral ground," which even they had to concede was not part of the terms of the treaty. The British argued that their occupation of this territory gave them the de facto right to it and the Anglo-American invasion of North Africa was supported by aircraft launched from Gibraltar.

No military assault against Gibraltar took place, but the war led Gibraltarians who lived and observed practices in Britain and elsewhere to both recognize their unique culture and to demand increased representation. The conflict in Gibraltar did not end in 1945, when World War II ended, but emerged as a major issue. Spain denounced the airstrip and other facilities on neutral ground, demanded the unconditional return of Gibraltar, imposed border restrictions, and then closed off the border entirely on June 8, 1969. The border was more fluid and arbitrary after World War II than it had been previously. The population also changed, first as a result of refugees from Spain during the Spanish Civil War and then from the forced evacuation of civilians after the outbreak of World War II. These years of trouble and the subsequent crisis when Franco closed the border, caused great strain initially, but ultimately forged a stronger community of Gibraltarians and increased their loyalty to Britain.

In the years between World War I and World War II, Gibraltar seemed to be increasingly vulnerable. The advent of planes and the improvements that made bombardment on a massive scale effective countered the value of Gibraltar as an impregnable fortress or as a base for the British Navy. The fortress itself could probably be bombed into submission with the new heavy artillery that could be fired long distances. Even if Spain was neutral and the fortress itself was not attacked, it would have to be supplied at least partially by sea. The harbor of Gibraltar, which had been enclosed by a wall, was now extremely vulnerable to aerial bombardment. In addition, the introduction of submarines meant that Gibraltar could no longer effectively monitor potential threats to the British Navy, into and out of the Mediterranean, as demonstrated by the 13 German submarines that had avoided detection while leaving the Mediterranean in 1918. It did not seem in 1920 as though Gibraltar would have a very great role to play in a future European conflict, but despite all the tensions and changes in the interwar years, Gibraltar did play a significant role in World War II.

The changes and advancements in technology were not the only ones during the interwar years. Changes in politics took place, as well. The general disillusionment that followed World War I—economic instability in Germany, Italy, and throughout Europe, as well as the inability to successfully integrate returning soldiers into society—led to the rise and growth of radical political parties. These nationalistic parties, such as Benito Mussolini's Fascist Party in Italy and Adolf Hitler's Nationalist Socialist German Workers Party in Germany, represented a threat to the peace that had been established after the war.

The threat of war increased the strategic importance of the Mediterranean. Britain would be hampered in fighting a war if the Strait of Gibraltar or the shipping routes through the Mediterranean and the Suez Canal were dangerous or closed.

Since the British gained control of Gibraltar in the early 1700s, the border between Spain and Gibraltar has not been clearly defined. This "No Man's Land" between Gibraltar and Spain stretches for 3/4 miles and is patrolled by both British and Spanish forces, which are pictured here in 1936.

Although diplomatic exchanges and international events posed a threat to Gibraltar, as late as 1935 the border dispute did not disrupt the ties that were established between Gibraltar and Spain. By the late 1930s, however, when it looked as if war might break out in Europe again, events in Spain had a direct impact on the population of Gibraltar and seemed to suggest that Britain might lose possession of "the Rock."

At the time, Gibraltar benefited Britain economically. In 1935, the British Department of Overseas Trade issued a report on economic conditions in Cyprus and Malta, which contained a brief assessment of the trade carried out on Gibraltar:

> The proximity of Gibraltar to Spain, the close connection existing between many Gibraltarian and Spanish people, the

common language, and the fact that Spanish papers are widely read in Gibraltar, all combine to influence the Gibraltar market to an appreciable extent. Goods which are known in Spain reap the benefit of that knowledge in Gibraltar also, and while this statement applies to many United Kingdom products, it is probably more generally applicable in the case of Continental articles. . . . Imports of *tobacco and cigarettes* are very large, and come almost entirely from the United Kingdom. They are largely re-exported.[72]

This report acknowledges the close ties between Spain and the population of Gibraltar. There had been no real or absolute border since the last Spanish siege of Gibraltar, and whatever hostility existed at the national level, it was not sufficient to deter ties between people who lived nearby to one another. Despite the artificial designation of a political border, there was no specific geographic division, and language, culture, and traditions in Gibraltar reflected those in Spain, although Spaniards in Gibraltar were affected by British customs and lived under British law. The innocuous statement that tobacco imports are very large and that they are largely reexported, is a reference to the continuation of illegal trade. The concerns of the Spanish state, including illegal trade and the political separation of Gibraltar from Spain, were very different from the concerns of individuals living in proximity to Gibraltar who stood to benefit from its economic prosperity.

Although British diplomacy before and during the Great War had brought Italy into the war on the side of the Allies and kept Spain neutral, there were long-term repercussions of Spain's stance. Spain had not fought with the Allies and had in fact given considerable assistance and material aid to the Germans; thus, Britain's refusal to consider the issue of Gibraltar or other grievances after the war might seem justifiable. Britain's statement to the effect that territory could not be returned to Spain because it was too weak and might let it fall into the hands of an enemy of Great Britain, led to a further deterioration of relations between Britain and Spain. The reference to Spain's weakness was seen as another insult and indicated British unwillingness to discuss the return of Gibraltar, just as the situation in Spain was about to change.[73]

Spain had a constitutional monarchy in 1895 following a brief and unsuccessful attempt to establish a republic. Although instability continued, with an extremely high number of changes in ministers and cabinets between 1895 and 1923, the system still functioned and a regent or king exercised power until Primo de Rivera established a dictatorship in 1923. In 1930, the army no longer supported Rivera, and he resigned. A temporary committee headed by General Damaso Berenguer tried to return Spain to a constitutional monarchy, but a revolution erupted instead. King Alfonso XIII agreed to leave Spain, and did so on April 14, 1931, but refused to formally abdicate the throne. The Second Republic was proclaimed and ruled from 1931 to 1936. Economic and social problems continued to plague Spain, which was also experiencing political instability as control of the government passed from left to right.

In 1936, the Popular Front (a coalition of democrats, socialists, and revolutionaries) assumed control of the government. The army and other conservatives who had become increasingly critical of the Republican government refused to accept the Popular Front. Led by an army general, Francisco Franco, they revolted, and civil war ensued. The civil war and Franco's victory seriously affected the dispute between Britain and Spain over Gibraltar.

Franco's victory undermined Spanish efforts to secure the return of Gibraltar. Franco was accused of extreme brutality during the civil war, including the destruction of the city of Guernica, carried out by the German Luftwaffe (air force) but authorized by Franco. The brutality of the war was apparent in Gibraltar, where the civilians, some of whom had relatives in Spain, watched the horrors of the war and admitted refugees from Spain.[74]

Aside from negative reactions to the brutal and authoritarian system by which Franco ruled Spain, the ties between Spain,

Germany, and Italy had grave implications when World War II began in 1939. Britain and France declared war on Germany after it invaded Poland. The fall of Poland in September 1939 and the collapse of France in 1940 left Britain waging war on her own against Germany and Italy, which had entered the war just prior to the collapse of France. The strained relationship between Britain and Spain, combined with Spain's ties to the Axis Powers, made it seem probable that Spain might enter the

FRANCISCO FRANCO

Francisco Paulino Hermenegildo Teodulo Franco y Bahamonde Salgado Pardo, generally referred to as Generalisimo Francisco Franco, was born in Ferrol, Spain, in 1892. Although other members of his family had served in the navy, Franco joined the army because military cutbacks prevented his joining the navy. He obtained a transfer to Morocco and joined the fighting there as soon as he was able to arrange it. As a result of his actions and his command of the Spanish Foreign Legion, he was promoted to general at the young age of 32 in 1926. After the fall of the monarchy in 1931, Franco served under the Republic and under the Popular Front, which came to power in February 1936. In July of that year, Franco joined the army uprising against the government and by October he was the head of the insurgent, or Nationalist, movement that was fighting for control of Spain in a bloody civil war.

Franco consolidated his control, and the Nationalist political parties and the Falange (the Spanish right wing "Fascist" organization) were integrated. Franco received economic assistance from Italy and Germany, and German aircraft and Italian ground forces operated in Spain. Franco won the Spanish Civil War and emerged as the Caudillo, or leader, of Spain in 1939. His victory was partly a result of German and Italian intervention and he remained linked to the "Axis" powers during World War II, but Spain remained neutral and did not allow German forces to use Spain as the base for an assault on Gibraltar. Although Franco did not attack or support an attack on Gibraltar, he clearly and forcefully expressed his views, similar to what Queen Isabella expressed war. To outsiders it seemed as though Franco would seize this opportunity to assist the countries that enabled him to win the civil war and regain the "key to Spain" at the same time. Initially, however, Franco declared Spanish neutrality and argued that Spain was too devastated by the civil war to enter into another conflict.

The British were acutely aware that Gibraltar's surrender would be an almost inevitable consequence of Spanish entry

in her will, to the effect that Spain must secure for all times the "key to Spain."

After the war, Franco and Spain were diplomatically isolated because of the links to the defeated nations of Germany and Italy, and also due to the authoritarian nature of the Franco regime. The emergence of the cold war enabled Franco to establish friendly relations with the United States, and Spain was subsequently admitted into the United Nations, an international peacekeeping body established in 1945. Spain immediately raised the issue of Gibraltar, and a UN recommendation advised Britain to resolve the conflict by directly negotiating with Spain. This apparent victory for Franco and Spain became meaningless, because Britain refused to negotiate and had promised Gibraltarians that it would not transfer sovereignty of the country against their wishes.

The economy of Spain improved and the political situation was fairly stable; thus, Franco launched an all-out campaign denouncing British occupation of territory belonging to Spain. After Queen Elizabeth II visited "the Rock" in 1954, Franco imposed border restrictions and ultimately sealed off the border between Spain and Gibraltar, severing phone lines and suspending ferry services. Franco's actions and his characterization of the population as criminals and displaced British citizens created a reaction in Gibraltar, and the hardships endured by the border-closing further hardened attitudes. The citizens of Gibraltar, even after Franco's death and the establishment of a democracy under the Bourbon Prince Juan Carlos, remain adamantly opposed even to joint sovereignty, let alone the transfer of Gibraltar to Spain.

As this overhead view of Gibraltar illustrates, British warships docked in its harbor were susceptible to air strikes during World War II. Fortunately for the British, the Spanish refused to let the Germans use their airbases during the war; consequently, Gibraltar was not subject to extensive bombing.

into the war. Of the two new weapons—submarines and aircraft—that played a large role in World War II, only one posed a significant threat. Even though submarines could enter the Mediterranean unnoticed and sink British ships, they could not attack ships in the Gibraltar harbor or shell the fortress. Airplanes, on the other hand, could render the position untenable by heavy bombardment. Gibraltar was bombed during the war, but it never endured a heavy or systematic bombardment, nor did heavy guns from the Spanish mainland ever fire upon the fortress. Although Spain remained inactive, the British dug extensive tunnels into "the Rock," set up an elaborate system of water collection, and evacuated all civilians who could not actively assist in the defense. Nevertheless, these measures could not change the fact that the docking facilities and, in all likelihood the fortress itself, were incapable of withstanding extensive bombardment.[75]

In 1940, Spain constructed a defensive line within a radius of 20 miles of Gibraltar, in case Britain decided to attack Spain to secure Gibraltar. The British continued construction of an airfield and used Gibraltar as a base for several ships, including a battleship, a cruiser, and nine destroyers. As long as the war was solely against Germany, and Spain remained neutral, the threat to Gibraltar seemed minimal. By May 1940, though, Belgium and France were on the verge of collapse, and Italy seemed poised to enter the war. Britain evacuated civilians from Gibraltar and the only inhabitants allowed to remain were about 4,000 able-bodied men who could assist in its defense.[76]

Even more so in World War II than in World War I, the most Britain could hope was that Spain would remain neutral. According to the new British prime pinister, Winston Churchill:

> All we wanted was the neutrality of Spain. We wanted to trade with Spain. We wanted her ports to be denied to German and Italian submarines. We wanted not only an unmolested Gibraltar, but the use of the anchorage of Algeciras for our ships and the use of the ground which joins the Rock to the mainland for our ever expanding airbase. On these facilities depended in large measure our access to the Mediterranean.[77]

Churchill noted that Spain, by merely mounting a dozen heavy guns in Algeciras, could render the British naval and air bases on Gibraltar useless. Churchill stated that Spain "held the key" to the Mediterranean because of its ability to prevent Britain from using "the Rock" as a base from which to support its operations in that sea.[78]

The Germans were also aware of the vulnerability of Gibraltar, if Spain could be convinced to join or support the Axis war effort. In order to defeat Britain, Germany could either directly launch an assault, as it did unsuccessfully during the Battle of Britain, or it could reduce British trade to such an extent that Britain would be forced to negotiate. Therefore, as soon as it became clear that the air attack against Britain had failed and that an invasion was unfeasible, the neutralization or capture of Gibraltar became the most likely alternative to produce a British surrender. As Gibraltar became more of a priority to the Germans, they pressured Spain and Franco to participate in the war or at least allow German troops passage through Spain.[79]

As a conservative army general, Franco had inherited the traditional nationalistic view of Gibraltar as an integral part of Spain. In 1939, he was still consolidating his control over Spain and attempting to revitalize a country devastated by war. Franco argued that any hostile act by Spain would prompt a blockade by Britain and that Spain could then only feed its population by importing foodstuffs and would not have the necessary materials to contribute to the war. Spain's reaction to the Italian declaration of war was to indicate that Spain was a "nonbelligerent" (or, not directly at war). This produced a considerable reaction in Britain, where it was noted that Mussolini had moved Italy from neutrality, to nonbelligerency, to war against the Allies.

Franco entered into talks with Germany and Italy that would have brought Spain into the war on the condition that all necessary materials and food would be provided by the Axis Powers. Franco, in fact, offered to enter the war in 1940, just before the collapse of France. There is considerable debate over Franco's intentions and whether his offer to enter the war on the Axis side was made in good faith, but it is a debate too extensive to fully discuss here. The reason Franco, despite his ardent nationalism, did not attack Gibraltar or allow the Germans to use Spain as a launching point for an attack, however, is relevant to the dispute over Gibraltar.

By 1940, the Spanish were shouting "Gibraltar for Spain," and Franco was making speeches about the necessity of assuming control of Gibraltar in order to create national unity. Franco, however, also signed an economic agreement with Britain in July 1940. The economic recovery of Spain was more important in the short term than the restoration of Gibraltar. Although Franco demanded the return of Gibraltar in the same nationalistic terms as earlier Spanish leaders, he was more of a pragmatist. Franco wanted a strong and economically prosperous Spain, and when he offered to enter the war on Germany's side in 1940, he demanded a substantial amount of economic aid in addition to his demands for Gibraltar and French territory in Northwest Africa.[80]

Hitler did not look favorably on Spain's offer to enter the war in return for significant concessions just as France was about to surrender. However, by August 1940, the situation had changed. Britain continued to wage war, and Hitler was planning the 1941 invasion of the Soviet Union. Gibraltar now assumed an importance in German planning that it had not had earlier. Once Germany launched its invasion eastward and became involved in a major effort there, Northwest Africa would be vulnerable to an attack by Britain. If Germany could seize Gibraltar and close the Strait of Gibraltar, then it would have made it more difficult for the British to launch an assault against North or Northwest Africa.

According to historian Norman J. W. Goda, Franco's negotiations with Hitler and the Germans not only failed to persuade him to join the war but convinced him that Spain must take whatever risks necessary to remain neutral. Goda argues that Franco had two primary aims. One was economic recovery and a national renewal that would allow Spain to regain its status as a major European power; the second was to regain Gibraltar and possibly expand Spanish territory in North Africa. As long as Germany wanted Spain's participation in the war and would seize Gibraltar in order to defeat Britain, Franco was willing to consider entering the war. He was not willing to sacrifice Spain's independence or economic recovery solely to regain Gibraltar, however much he might desire its return. Thus, in early negotiations with Hitler, Franco wanted a promise of Spain's independence and also to secure the necessary supplies to maintain its economic recovery. [81]

During the negotiations that took place in August 1940 and during the meeting at Hendaye, France, according to Goda,

German representatives, including Hitler, began to discuss Gibraltar in different terms. The Germans suggested that Gibraltar and Northwest Africa were the key not just to the defeat of Britain but to Germany's ability to wage war against other nations such as the United States, and that possession of these territories might be the first step in the establishment of a Greater German Empire. Goda argues that as soon as Franco concluded that the Germans were interested in the possession of Gibraltar in and of itself and not as a means to defeat Britain, he became determined to remain neutral and prevent the German seizure of Gibraltar. Franco considered Gibraltar to be Spanish territory and had no interest in its transfer to any other foreign power, especially one as strong as Germany appeared to be in 1940.[82]

During 1940 and 1941, the British still viewed the threat to Gibraltar as imminent and tried to secure Spain's neutrality by assisting Franco in the only way they could. Britain provided food and credit to Spain, and Churchill managed, through great personal effort, to convince the American president, Franklin D. Roosevelt, to assist Spain. The United States provided 100,000 tons of wheat to Spain as a gift. Even after Britain had been informed about the Hendaye meeting and rightly assumed that Spain would not enter the war, it was still possible that Germany might send forces through Spain and thus the threat remained.[83]

By 1942, Spain was still neutral, although it was providing more direct assistance to German submarines than it had during World War I, by allowing them to resupply in Spanish harbors. Britain assumed that Spain would not assault "the Rock," as long as it was not at war. However, Gibraltar remained vulnerable to air attack, and as late as July 1942, Churchill believed that the Germans could continue the war in the Soviet Union and send a force to occupy Portugal and Spain. The British ultimately decided that the only real solution was to acquire harbors and overland routes in North Africa, so British supply lines could still function if Germany occupied Spain and seized Gibraltar.

During World War II, Germany had designs on capturing Gibraltar and Northwest Africa, because it believed by controlling the gateway to the Mediterranean, it would have a better chance of defeating both Great Britain and the United States. However, General Francisco Franco, who is pictured here shaking hands with Adolf Hitler in 1940, remained neutral throughout the war and did not help Germany achieve its goal of capturing Gibraltar.

Spain, however, was the key to this plan, because the British had convinced the United States that Gibraltar should be used as the launching point for the Anglo-American invasion of North Africa, code-named Operation Torch. President Roosevelt was very concerned about the question of Spain and on August 26, 1942, Churchill sent another letter reassuring Roosevelt that the operation could be successfully launched from Gibraltar: "In my view, it would be reasonable to assume (a) that Spain will not go to war with Britain and the United States on account of "Torch"; (b) that it will be at least two months before the Germans can force their way through Spain or procure some accommodation from her."[84]

Up to this point, Britain had needed Spain's neutrality only to keep Gibraltar from Germany. Now, however, in order to carry out Operation Torch, Spain would have to exhibit benevolent neutrality or be willing to ignore the buildup of Allied forces in a territory adjoining Spain. Britain would be violating the Treaty of Utrecht by using the neutral ground in its operations. Churchill was also extremely concerned that Spain might either pass along information to the Germans or that the Germans might become aware of Allied activity and demand that Spain force Britain to evacuate the neutral ground or to allow the Germans to place aircraft on Spanish territory for operations against Gibraltar.

The arbitrary nature of the border thus affected British strategy and plans during World War II. Britain could occupy the ground in front of the fortress, but since this territory had not been officially ceded, it always constituted a risk. Officially, Britain had no right to the territory, and Spain, which had consistently and bitterly opposed any military operations or defensive positions in this area, might be provoked into a military response. Britain was in a rather precarious position during most of World War II and could not afford to provoke Spain. An official line of demarcation might have limited the use of Gibraltar as a base for launching operations against North Africa, but these operations would have been far less risky if an official border existed.

The British Embassy in Madrid reassured Churchill, essentially indicating that it was extremely unlikely that Franco would accede to German demands. Furthermore, it was clear that the acquisition of North Africa could be of vital importance to the war effort. Gibraltar had only been useful in assembling aircraft to be flown to Malta, which was the vital base that enabled the British to maintain their presence in the Mediterranean. Gibraltar could not keep Malta from succumbing to an attack, a fact demonstrated by the heavy losses of aircraft and ships that convoys from Gibraltar to Malta had sustained.

Nevertheless, on November 5, 1942, it was Gibraltar and not Malta that played a crucial role in the war. U.S. General Dwight D. Eisenhower landed on "the Rock" and, from the airfield on the neutral ground, launched the bombardment that preceded the Anglo-American invasion of Northwest Africa. The successful invasion of Northwest Africa and defeat of Axis forces in North Africa was followed by the invasion of Sicily in 1943. The landings on Sicily, and then mainland Italy, removed any possibility that Germany would invade Spain or assault Gibraltar. After the invasion of Normandy in June 1944, Gibraltar ceased to be involved in World War II.

Although the British began to transport back the residents of Gibraltar who had been evacuated, there were not enough ships available to accomplish the tasks, in part because of the continuation of the war in the Pacific. It took a long time for the civilian evacuees to be returned, but the war was over and Britain, which had seemed in grave danger of losing both Gibraltar and the war, had emerged victorious. In the aftermath of World War II, a number of issues, including the dispute between Britain and Spain over Gibraltar, reemerged.

At the end of World War II, Franco stated that Gibraltar was Spain's territory and demanded its return. Meanwhile, Britain, France, and the United States refused to allow Spain to join the United Nations or to provide assistance to Franco, who had helped Germany and who was viewed as a Fascist. Spain's claim to Gibraltar might have had little effect if decolonization had not been hastened by the decline of Britain and France after World War II. The question of Gibraltar soon garnered international attention, however, and Britain came under pressure from the United Nations to resolve this issue.

During World War II, Franco had been unwilling to break completely with either the Axis or the Allies, and this had effectively placed restraints upon his policies and official statements. After the war, Spain was diplomatically isolated and suffered from an economic recession, but it was still in a stronger position than during the war. Accordingly, Franco became increasingly vocal about the continued occupation of Spanish territory (Gibraltar). He denounced the airfield that had been constructed on territory retained by Spain under the terms of the treaty ceding Gibraltar. The return of the civilian population and the demand for increased self-government caused Spain to cite Article X of the Treaty of Peace and Friendship and demand Gibraltar's return (a familiar tactic), but it also led to a debate on the legitimacy of the civilian community and on whether a border could or should exist between Gibraltar and the Iberian mainland.

6

Franco, the United Nations, and Gibraltar, 1945–1975

Spain emerged from World War II having escaped the devastation experienced by countries that were invaded or occupied by Nazi Germany, but it faced considerable challenges in the postwar world. Franco's authoritarian dictatorship and Spain's dealings with the Axis Powers resulted in the diplomatic isolation of Spain in the aftermath of a war fought to preserve democracy. Spain's economy was faltering, it was denied membership in the United Nations in 1946, and in March of that year the United States, Britain, and France expressed their desire that the Franco regime would make way for democratic reforms in Spain. It was hardly a good time for Spain to demand the return of Gibraltar, but Franco stated it as his utmost priority. There were no normal diplomatic channels available for discussions, because Britain had withdrawn its ambassador from Madrid and did not allow Spain to have an ambassador in London as part of a policy—initiated by the Soviets but warmly received by the former Allies—of excluding Spain from the international community.[85]

In the immediate aftermath of World War II, Britain simply ignored Franco's demands that Gibraltar be returned to Spain. The British believed that it was Franco personally who desired the return of "the Rock." The British, who hoped that the isolation of Spain would lead to the fall of Franco's regime, assumed that the issue of Gibraltar would recede as soon as Franco fell from power. This attitude by Britain was based on entirely false assumptions. In demanding the return of Gibraltar, Franco was echoing the position of every Spanish government since the loss of Gibraltar in 1704. He was not the originator of the idea that Gibraltar was Spanish territory unlawfully occupied by a foreign power; his views represented a culmination of the attitudes and beliefs that had been passed down for centuries in Spain.

The entire population of Spain had been outraged by the loss of the "key to Spain" and despite regional differences and internal divisions, there remained an extraordinary degree of consensus on the Spanish view of "the Rock." During the most

Shortly after the end of World War II in 1945, Francisco Franco became increasingly vocal about Great Britain's continued occupation of Gibraltar. Despite his blustering, Franco was never able to retake Gibraltar and the territory remains in British hands.

glorious pinnacle in the history of Spain, Gibraltar was conquered and Spain was unified under the monarchy. This process was completed with the final expulsion of Jews and Moors in 1492, and the following century witnessed the expansion of Spain and the establishment of a vast colonial empire. Gibraltar, where the British allowed Jews and Moors to settle, symbolized the decline of Spanish power and the superiority of Britain. In addition to the decline of Spain as a great power, Gibraltar represented the humiliation of losing an integral part of Spain connected to the mainland. Ernle Bradford argues that the policies of the Franco regime stem directly from "that insult to Spanish pundonor, or 'point of honour,' which the foreign occupation represented."[86]

Gibraltar was Spanish territory occupied by a foreign power, and its immediate return was the fervent desire of every Spaniard. Student demonstrations and attacks on British corporations and its embassy building (which remained, although there was no current ambassador) in Spain were attributed to Franco but represented the outrage of Spanish students over the British possession of Gibraltar. Franco further consolidated his control and was named chief of state for life on March 31, 1947, but he could not bring Gibraltar or any other issue before the international community, as Spain continued to be excluded from this arena.

The situation for Spain, and by extension for Gibraltar, was altered by the deepening of the cold war between the United States and the Soviet Union. A conflict between the wartime allies had emerged with regard to the postwar peace settlement and the Soviet occupation of Eastern Europe. As tensions increased and the United States sought to contain the Soviet Union and Communist ideology, it began to look for additional allies in Europe. Franco's authoritarian regime and his relationship with the Fascist nations had led to his international isolation, but his staunch anti-Communist policies led to Spain's reentry into the international community. Franco had denounced Communism both before and during the Spanish

Civil War, when the Soviet Union had assisted the anti-Franco forces. Franco had continually argued that Communism represented a threat to Europe, and a division of Spanish volunteers had fought alongside the German forces against the Soviet Union. In December 1950, as a result of the outbreak of the Korean War, and the perceived threat posed by the Soviet Union to Western Europe, the United States recognized the Franco regime. Britain and France also recognized the Spanish government, and that same year, the issue of Gibraltar reemerged.

As a result of negotiations begun in 1944, Gibraltar was granted a legislative council in 1950 with voting by proportional representation. Although it was far from a democratic system, since 5 of the 10 members were from the official British establishment and the military governor had the tie-breaking vote, it was a measure of self-representation. Spain objected to the changes in the administration of Gibraltar and argued that they were largely in appearance and did not change the reality of the colonial status. Britain responded that it had indicated to the United Nations in 1946 that Gibraltar was a non-self-governing territory, and as such it was now carrying out changes in line with the attitude and policies established by the UN General Assembly to promote decolonization. Prince Philip, Duke of Edinburgh, visited Gibraltar in 1950 and stated that Britain's long-term goal was for the territory to become self-governing. Nevertheless, Spain officially demanded the return of Gibraltar and denounced British intentions to grant the colony independence.

This initial demand was another instance of Spain's attempt to use the wording of the Treaty of Peace and Friendship to secure the return of the territory. Article X stated that Britain had to first offer Gibraltar to Spain if it decided "to grant, sell or by any means to alienate therefrom the propriety of the said town of Gibraltar."[87] Spain was on firmer ground than some of its assertions based on the more vaguely worded passages of the Article X because of the phrase "by any means to alienate." The broad nature of this term makes it quite easy and logical to argue that granting independence is in fact alienating or separating Gibraltar from Britain in some way and therefore Britain must allow Spain the opportunity to acquire the territory before proceeding. The British did not directly respond to this issue but instead emphasized that the international community and the United Nations have advocated decolonization and that granting greater self-governance to Gibraltar meets this criteria, whereas transferring it to Spain violates the wishes of the population.

Gibraltar's population was greatly affected by World War II and was increasingly involved in the dispute over the future status of the territory. During the war, with the exception of about 4,000 able-bodied men, the civilian population had been forcibly evacuated by the British. Families were separated, some evacuees were moved more than once, and some were sent as far away as Australia. Those Gibraltarians who had lived in London during the war were isolated and treated as inferior by many British citizens. In 1944, after the invasion of Normandy, British citizens returned to claim their homes, and about 10,000 evacuees in London were moved to empty army huts outside Belfast, where they waited to be returned to Gibraltar.

Their return was delayed by the shortage of available ships, and some had to wait five years for transport. Some of these individuals had contact with natives from other British colonies, such as India and Ireland, and they became aware of the process by which these countries had gained concessions from Britain. Since Gibraltar could not become self-sustaining due to a lack of natural resources, complete independence was not a feasible or even desirable goal. The aim of Gibraltarians was to force the British Colonial Office to allot substantial sums of money for the construction of additional housing and hospitals, and the improvement of the educational system.

The legislative council had been a concession to the demands of the population, which also wanted the British government to invest money in the economy. There was some anti-British sentiment in Gibraltar after World War II, but actions taken by Franco's government soon eliminated these tensions, and the

British and Gibraltarians presented a unified front. Franco instructed Spanish newspapers to print demands for the return of Gibraltar, and they complied. Those Gibraltarians who had lived elsewhere during the war had become aware of their unique culture and outlook and had also become extremely sensitive to criticism, in part because they were treated as greatly inferior by other British nationals. They were offended by Spanish newspaper reports and radio broadcasts, beginning in 1951, which portrayed all Gibraltarians as criminals with unsavory pasts.

Spanish newspapers chose to ignore the very real ties and influence of Spanish culture on the population of Gibraltar: "They pursued for the next 15 years a totally counterproductive pattern of speaking disparagingly of the Gibraltarians, and lost Spain the best chance in 100 years of winning over a community less different from its neighbors than its neighbors were from the Spanish communities of Aragon or Castile."[88] While Spain was denouncing the character of the population and insisting that Gibraltar was essentially a military garrison and the rightful territory of Spain, Britain was providing money and improving living conditions on "the Rock."

By this time, the population had ceased to be arbitrary in nature, but the border had not. During periods when the border restrictions were not imposed, there was a great deal of interaction between the population of Gibraltar and Spain. There were cultural differences arising from British rule and law and customs, but it was impossible to eliminate the influence of Spanish and Mediterranean culture on "the Rock," and the inhabitants reflected these customs to some extent and would have reflected them to a greater extent if Spain had not frequently closed the border.

The standard of living improved on Gibraltar, and there was a marked difference between conditions there and those in the nearest Spanish town, La Linea, which was extremely poor. The citizens of Gibraltar could hardly be faulted for preferring to remain as dependents of a British nation that was investing considerable sums of money in the colony, instead of being under

For many years after World War II, Spain's economy suffered greatly. As a result, towns such as La Linea, which lies on the eastern isthmus of the Bay of Algeciras, were very poor, while Gibraltar's economy continued to thrive under British control. Gibraltar is pictured here from La Linea, which is just to the north of "the Rock."

the control of a Spanish nation that disparaged their culture and that did not seem to have the financial resources to support them.

As discussed in Chapter 1, Queen Elizabeth II visited Gibraltar in 1954, and the people of Gibraltar gave her a genuinely warm welcome, despite previous grievances. This visit was protested by Spanish authorities and labeled as "a deliberate act of defiance by [the queen's] government."[89] Spain implemented a policy that it described as a stricter compliance with the Treaty of Utrecht and prohibited Spanish citizens without a justifiable reason from traveling to Gibraltar, closing the Spanish consulate on "the Rock."

After Spain imposed border restrictions, diplomatic negotiations between Britain and Spain reached a complete impasse. The British would not discuss the issue of transfer of sovereignty or any other issue related to Gibraltar unless Spain lifted the border restrictions. Spain refused to do so until the British were willing to discuss granting independence to Gibraltar and its transfer to Spain. Since neither side was willing to enter negotiations without gaining a concession that the other side refused to make, the situation was gridlocked.

In 1955, Spain gained entry into the international diplomatic community when it was admitted to the United Nations. Despite the impasse, or possibly because there were no ongoing discussions regarding Gibraltar, Anglo-Spanish relations improved toward the end of the 1950s. Economic problems in Spain demanded the attention of its government, and, by necessity, Gibraltar became a lower priority. Spain became increasingly involved in international economic affairs, and its new policies—including reduced restrictions on foreign investment, increased trade, and obtaining of international support grants— meant that Spain and Britain were brought into contact with one another.

The Spanish minister, Fernando de Castiella, made an official visit to London in 1960, and in 1961, the British foreign minister, Lord Home, went to Madrid. Both countries stressed the potential benefits of a harmonious relationship, not just for their own countries but for all of Europe. Lord Home stressed that, in the effort to improve and maintain better relations, the two countries should proceed slowly and not force immediate resolutions to problems that might be difficult to solve. Whether or not he was referring to Gibraltar, renewed attempts to resolve the Gibraltar question eventually led once again to the deterioration of relations between Britain and Spain.[90]

The dispute over Gibraltar entered a new phase after 1963, when Spain requested that the UN Special Committee of 24 on Decolonization, which dealt with bringing colonialism to an end, consider the issue of Gibraltar. On September 11, 1963, the British presented a report to the committee, which initially addressed the amount the United Kingdom had expended since 1946 on facilities such as the docks and airstrip, as well as social services such as new housing. The British report concluded with a paragraph indicating that the people of Gibraltar wished to remain associated with Britain and that the British government would abide by their wishes and would consider any further changes requested by the elected representatives of the Gibraltarians.[91]

Spain responded for the first time. During previous meetings in which Gibraltar had been discussed, Spain had "reserved its rights" in the matter or essentially passed on the opportunity to issue a statement or report. In 1963, Spain submitted its own report to the Special Committee, insisting that Gibraltar was still Spanish territory and thus the division represented an artificial border, not a real border between two legitimate states or nations. Spain also refused to recognize the population of Gibraltar as a legitimate community with rights and a legitimate voice in any proceedings that would affect the status of the territory. The Spanish minister for foreign affairs, Don Fernando Maria de Castiella, described the Gibraltar situation in the following terms during talks on the status of Gibraltar held in London in May 1964:

> The present inhabitants of Gibraltar were an artificially constituted aggregate which basically altered the original bilateral relationship between Britain and Spain. This third party [Gibraltarians] was not valid because Gibraltar was merely a military base which belonged to either the country which occupied it or to the country in whose territory it existed, but not to a third party. Nor did the inhabitants have any real or profound link between the territory and themselves, because they were fabricated by the colonial power to satisfy the needs of the military base. . . . Gibraltar's economy was based on smuggling, because it lacked the requisite resources and size for the development of a normal economy. As a consequence of those limitations, Spain suffered the noxious effects of this illicit trade. In addition, Gibraltar had no labor force of its own; therefore, colonial exploitation of Spanish workers existed."[92]

Spain argued that, since the inhabitants of Gibraltar did not represent a true community, the UN resolution that applied was resolution 1514(XV) on decolonization, which included a point emphasizing that "any attempt aimed at the partial or total disruption of the national unity and the territorial integrity of a country is incompatible with the purposes and principles of the Charter of the United Nations."[93] Spain's position rested on the premise that the territory most affected by the British colony of Gibraltar was Spain. The territorial integrity of Spain had been compromised and the legitimate population had left in 1704, as a result of the British conquest. In this context, the return of Gibraltar to Spain despite the wishes of the population could be justified.

Sir Joshua Hassan and Peter Isola, two members of Gibraltar's representative council, rejected the Spanish argument, saying that some families had been living there for more than 100 years, and the blending of Spanish and British influences had resulted in a unique culture, which does not support the Spanish view of a recently transplanted British community.[94] The Gibraltarians referred to Article 73 of Chapter XI of the UN Charter, which states that member states must allow for the emergence of self-government in areas under their control. The Gibraltarians also noted resolution 1541(XV), which includes several principles for determining whether or not a territory is non-self-governing and also states the ways in which the aim for such territories—of a full measure of self-government—can be achieved. According to this resolution,

> Principle VI
> A Non-Self-Governing Territory can be said to have reached a full measure of self-government by:
>> (a) Emergence as a sovereign independent State;
>> (b) Free association with an independent State; or
>> (c) Integration with an Independent State[95]

Gibraltarian representatives argued that one of the options described by the UN is "free association with an Independent State."[96] Therefore, the Gibraltarian desire to remain tied to

Sir Joshua Hassan (left), pictured here with then-governor of Gibraltar Sir Gerald Lathbury, served as chief minister of Gibraltar from 1964 to 1969 and again from 1972 to 1987. Hassan was instrumental in helping to grant Gibraltar limited self-representation, but he never considered complete independence feasible or even desirable.

Britain, rather than choosing independence or integration with Spain, is valid and should be accepted. The key issue turned out to be the question of whether the people of Gibraltar represent a true community or are merely a function of the British military base. If Gibraltar is primarily a military base with a dependent settlement, then the resolution on the territorial integrity of nations should take precedence and Gibraltar should be returned to Spain. If the town of Gibraltar is independent of the garrison, however, with a unique cultural blend of British and Spanish traditions, then it would seem that the population has a right to self-determination. If the right of people to determine their own form of government is the most important principle by which one settles the dispute, then Gibraltar should remain linked to Britain, as Gibraltarians apparently desire.

The British refused to acknowledge the claim of the Spanish government that it must be consulted on any changes in the constitution or status of Gibraltar. Britain maintained that the transfer of Gibraltar to her under the Treaty of Utrecht was absolute and therefore Britain could enact any measures it deemed appropriate. Britain did not consider the granting of a greater measure of independence to Gibraltar as an alienation of the territory.

Instead, the British emphasized that the implementation of a greater degree of independence for Gibraltarians was in full accord with the UN Charter and with resolutions such as 1541(XV) in regard to colonial or dependent territories. The tension and conflict between Gibraltarians and Britain had disappeared; they would present a united front to the United Nations as well as to Spain, and in doing so would strengthen their relationship. Britain assured the Gibraltarians that it would not transfer sovereignty against their wishes, and having given its word, refused to consider this as an option.

On October 16, 1963, the UN Committee reached a consensus and issued a statement containing several key points. It concluded that a dispute or disagreement over the status of Gibraltar existed and it encouraged Britain and Spain to participate in discussions to resolve this issue. The committee also said that the issue should be resolved by negotiating a solution that upheld the principles of Resolution 1514(XV), "and bearing in mind the interest of the population."[97]

The UN committee's pointed reference to resolution 1514(XV), which dealt with territorial integrity, and the fact that it omitted any reference to resolution 1541(XV), indicated that it had found the Spanish argument more compelling. Although the committee suggested bilateral negotiations between those countries, it did not state that the Gibraltarians should be involved. It only noted that their interests should be considered. Spain had successfully gained the support of the United Nations, in part because of the support of the representatives of Uruguay, Tunisia, and Venezuela, and also the suggestion by Iraq, Syria, and Cambodia that Spain and Britain should conduct negotiations. The British position was not altered by the views of the UN committee, however. Britain did not accept the authority or position of the UN and refused to discuss the question of sovereignty over Gibraltar.

Consequently, Spain imposed further restrictions on the passage of goods and individuals between Gibraltar and Spain. It announced its willingness to enter into negotiations and hinted that further restrictions might be imposed if the British refused to negotiate. Britain refused to enter into talks under pressure, and in March 1965, Spain introduced further restrictions that it openly acknowledged were a response to the British refusal to negotiate. The issue of Gibraltar came up again in UN discussions in December 1965, and again the UN urged Anglo-Spanish negotiations and said that it did not agree with the British view that the desire of the inhabitants should be the key factor in determining the future of the territory.

During the meeting, the UN advised Britain and Spain to resume negotiations and to keep the organization informed. In May 1966, the first of four rounds of talks were inaugurated at a meeting held in London. The Spanish delegation claimed sovereignty over "the Rock" and proposed a settlement based upon a four-point plan:

1. The signing of an Anglo-Spanish convention, the first Article of which should provide for the cancellation of Article X of the Treaty of Utrecht of 1713 and "the restoration of the national unity and territorial integrity of Spain through the reversion of Gibraltar."
2. The continuation of a British military base in Gibraltar "whose structure, legal situation, and coordination with the defence organization of Spain or the free world would be the subject of a special agreement attached to the convention."

3. The signing of an additional Anglo-Spanish agreement registered with the UN dealing with a legal regime protecting the interests of the present citizens of Gibraltar. In that agreement, in addition to the appropriate economic and administrative formulae, a personal statute would be established by which, among other fundamental rights—such as freedom of religion—the British nationality of the present inhabitants would be respected and their right of residence guaranteed, as would be the free exercise of their lawful activities and a guarantee of permanence in their place of work.

4. The effective date of the convention should come after the two additional agreements referred to in (2) and (3) above had been registered with the UN.[98]

Britain requested additional information on the status and protections offered Gibraltarians under this proposal, but its official response was that it would not negotiate on the sovereignty of Gibraltar. The response reassured Gibraltarians who were determined to remain associated with Great Britain and were unequivocally opposed to the transfer of the sovereignty to Spain under any terms or conditions. During the second round of talks, the British advanced a four-point proposal very different in nature from the one Spain had presented. Britain suggested that the internal self-government of Gibraltar be carried out by municipal authorities rather than an executive and legislative council. Britain also proposed that Spain could use the airport and docking facilities, that the Spanish government could appoint an official to oversee their interests in Gibraltar, and that Spain and Britain would work together to combat smuggling. The talks ended the flurry of notes that were exchanged between the two countries during the previous year, but they made little progress toward resolving the key issue of sovereignty.

In December 1967, the UN adopted a resolution in regard to Gibraltar. The UN demanded that Britain end the colonial situation in Gibraltar, set a deadline of October 1, 1969, by which Gibraltar should be decolonized, and again specified that Anglo-Spanish discussions should resume immediately. Lord Hugh Mackintosh Foot Caradon, the U.K. representative to the United Nations, told the General Assembly of that body that the resolution "will not and cannot be put into effect before adding that any attempt to force Britain to hand over the inhabitants of Gibraltar to Spain against their will was happily so removed from possibility as to be incredible."[99]

Despite the involvement of the United Nations, the problem remained insoluble. Britain introduced further constitutional changes in Gibraltar and continued to approve and provide millions of pounds for investment in the economy, which was greatly impacted by increasing Spanish restrictions on the passage of individuals and goods between Spain and Gibraltar. Spain also prohibited aircraft landing on Gibraltar to fly through Spanish air space, and as of 1969, completely closed its border with Gibraltar and cut communication lines. Further exchanges between Britain and Spain occurred, but the constitutional changes enacted in Gibraltar remained in place, the border remained sealed, and the dispute on the status of Gibraltar remained unresolved.

Through its actions, Spain not only achieved the opposite of its aims (the return of Gibraltar) by hardening British attitudes, but also transformed an arbitrary political border into a very real one. Closing the border completely separated Gibraltar from Spain, stopping the pattern of intermarriage and interactions between the populations of Spain and Britain, which had resulted from the permeable nature of the border. These interactions had undermined the artificial division of the isthmus into British and Spanish zones. Franco severed this connection and incurred not only the permanent ill-will of the Gibraltarians but also alienated Spaniards who could no longer work in Gibraltar and thus became unemployed.

As a result of the border closure, which lasted from 1969 until 1985, Gibraltar became more dependent on Britain and completely independent from Spain. The British government provided a substantial sum of money to alleviate the economic depression that resulted from the border closing. In 1974, Britain allotted more than £7.6 million (approximately $13.7 million) in capital aid to be distributed between 1975 and 1978 to increase Gibraltar's self-sufficiency.[100] Gibraltar had been under British rule for more than 300 years, and now its complete separation from Spain led its population to identify even further with Britain.

7

The Lisbon Agreement and Beyond

The death of Francisco Franco in 1975 led to changes in the
Spanish government. Juan Carlos, named by Franco as his
successor, became King Juan Carlos of Spain on November 22,
1975, and introduced democratic reforms. Spain also applied to
join the European Community (EC). British willingness to support this application led to renewed hopes that a settlement on
Gibraltar might be reached or that normal communication and
travel between Gibraltar and Spain might be restored. As barriers and restrictions between European countries were being
weakened and removed by membership in the EC, it seemed logical that the restoration of a permeable border between Gibraltar
and Spain might come about. The situation had been altered,
however, by the policies of the Franco regime and by the impact
of the closing of the border for such a long period.

The death of Franco did not have an immediate impact on
Gibraltar, although it was a factor in some political changes and
in the Gibraltar election in 1975, which produced little support
for those independents who had urged accommodation with
Spain. The population was still determined to remain closely
associated with Great Britain, and Spain continued to insist that
Gibraltar was Spanish territory and must be returned. Thus, the
accession of Juan Carlos to the throne of Spain and democratic
changes in Spain did not alter the status quo with regard to
Gibraltar. Nor did Spain relax the restrictions it had imposed
between Gibraltar and mainland Spain. Communication, travel,
and trade between Spain and Gibraltar were still forbidden.

Despite Spanish statements to the effect that the territorial
integrity of Spain was the primary aim of Spanish foreign policy, which was a clear reference to Gibraltar in light of the UN
recommendations, Anglo-Spanish relations did improve. Spain
indicated its desire to renew talks with Britain and formally submitted an application to the EC. The residents of Gibraltar,
under the leadership of Sir Joshua Hassan, grew concerned that
Britain might be willing to compromise on Gibraltar in
exchange for full Spanish participation in European affairs and
as a member of the anti-Soviet coalition. Not only did Britain

After the death of Francisco Franco in 1975, Spain's relationship with Gibraltar remained status quo: King Juan Carlos still supported a closed border between Spain and "the Rock." Franco and Juan Carlos are pictured here in June 1974 at a military parade during the thirty-fifth anniversary of the end of the Spanish Civil War.

support Spain's application to the European Community, but it also indicated it would support Spain's application to the North Atlantic Treaty Organization (NATO) and that it would *not* make its support conditional on Spanish concessions with regard to the blockade of Gibraltar. Spain insisted it would only consider removing the restrictions after the resumption of talks on the territorial status of Gibraltar but stressed that it would take the wishes of the population into account.

The actual discussions proceeded along well-established lines. Spain refused to reopen the border as a gesture of good-will or as an initial step, insisting that the regulations could only be lifted if progress was made on the key issue of the status of Gibraltar. The population of Gibraltar remained adamant that it would not accept any solution that involved the transfer of partial or full sovereignty to Spain under any conditions. The pattern with regard to the initiation and breakdown of negotiations repeated itself once again. In 1977, however, the Spanish authorities restored telephone communications during the Christmas period, and unlike 1975, the connection was not terminated at the end of the holiday season.

Also in 1977, the Spanish minister, Señor Marcelino Oreja Aguirre, said that "Spain prefers to look upon Gibraltar in a present day context and not in terms of the Treaty of Utrecht, if that is possible."[101] It was a startling statement, considering that all of Spain's previous efforts, except perhaps its claim that Gibraltar had never ceased to be Spain's territory, had been based on the terms of the Treaty of Utrecht or on British violations of the treaty. Spain now wanted to focus not on the past dispute and former agreements but on a future in which Britain and Spain would be closely connected as fellow members of the European Community.

Before discussions on Gibraltar could proceed further, however, Spain was embarrassed by international developments. King Hassan II of Morocco, as a result of a dispute over the Canary Islands, stated that, if Gibraltar was returned to Spain, then the ports of Ceuta and Melilla (both Spanish enclaves in North Africa) would have to be returned by Spain to Morocco. Britain was also becoming aware of the impact that the issue of Gibraltar had on its foreign policy and international relations. The proposed visit by King Juan Carlos to Britain, British support for Spain's entry into the EC, and the question of Spanish membership in NATO were three separate issues not directly related to the status of Gibraltar. They could not be raised or discussed, though, without the issue of Gibraltar also coming to the forefront, especially as Gibraltarians were very concerned that better relations between the two countries might cause Britain to consider a settlement contrary to their wishes. Spain's increasing role in the EC had significant long-term implications.

Gibraltar continued to figure in discussions, but no progress was made toward a resolution. Spain suggested in 1980 that, if Britain abided by the UN mandate to discuss the status of

Gibraltar, Spain might restore communications between Gibraltar and the Iberian Peninsula. The debate in Spain was influenced by the protests of Spaniards living in La Linea who had also been negatively affected by the closing of the "border." The Spanish statement was not fundamentally different than earlier statements of policy, but there appeared to be a new willingness to break the impasse and to begin real negotiations on the lifting of the restrictions and the future of Gibraltar. Talks were held between the British and Spanish foreign ministers in Lisbon in 1980 and actually resulted in a joint Anglo-Spanish statement, known as the Lisbon Agreement.

The agreement was indicative of the new spirit of cooperation that was established, but the conflicting views of the two parties appeared to remain. The Spanish minister, Señor Aguirre, emphasized that the rights of the Gibraltarians would be respected. The Gibraltarians' territorial independence from Spain was excluded from the guarantee, however, on the basis that territorial sovereignty had never belonged to them and thus could not be upheld. Gibraltar's chief minister and the head of the opposition met with British officials, though, and publicly supported the Lisbon Agreement and looked forward to the end of the restrictions, sometimes referred to as a "siege" of Gibraltar by Spain.

There was significant opposition to the agreement in Gibraltar, however. Even though the real benefits of negotiations based on this agreement would be reaped by the residents of Gibraltar, who would no longer be isolated, there were those willing to endure the continuation of these measures rather than affirm the agreement.

Many Gibraltarians who objected to the Lisbon Agreement were members of the Gibraltar Socialist Labour Party (GSLP), and they protested for a number of reasons directly related to the agreement itself or its wording. They noted, for instance, that the agreement was negotiated between Britain and Spain without the presence of a Gibraltarian representative. They also objected to the wording in the fourth clause, which stated that

THE LISBON AGREEMENT

The Lisbon Agreement, signed by Spain and Great Britain in 1980, reads as follows:

1. The British and Spanish Governments desiring to strengthen their bilateral relations and thus to contribute to Western solidarity, intend, in accordance with the relevant United Nations resolutions, to resolve in a spirit of friendship, the Gibraltar problem.

2. Both Governments have therefore agreed to start negotiations aimed at overcoming all the differences between them on Gibraltar.

3. Both Governments have reached agreement on the re-establishment of direct communications in the region. The Spanish Government has decided to suspend the application of measures at present in force. Both Governments have agreed that full co-operation should be on the basis of reciprocity and full equality of rights. They look forward to the further steps which will be taken on both sides which they believe will open the way to closer understanding between those directly concerned in the area.

4. To this end both Governments will be prepared to consider any proposals which the other may wish to make, recognising the need to develop practical co-operation on a mutually beneficial basis.

5. The Spanish Government, in reaffirming its position on the re-establishment of the territorial integrity of Spain, restated its intention that in the coming negotiations the interests of the Gibraltarians should be fully safeguarded. For its part the British Government will fully maintain its commitment to honour the freely and democratically expressed wishes of the people of Gibraltar as set out in the preamble to the (1969) Gibraltar Constitution.

6. Officials of both sides will meet as soon as possible to prepare the necessary practical steps which will permit the implementation of the proposals agreed to above. It is envisaged that these preparations will be completed no later than 1 June.[*]

[*] Peter Gold, *A Stone in Spain's Shoe: The Search for a Solution to the Problem of Gibraltar*. Liverpool, Great Britain: Liverpool University Press, 1994, pp. 92–93.

Despite the reopening of the border between Spain and Gibraltar in 1985, residents of Gibraltar continue to oppose Spain's desire to reclaim the territory. Gibraltarians overwhelmingly support British control of "the Rock" and oppose joint sovereignty.

both governments would discuss any proposal made by the other, saying this suggested that the British would, in direct contrast to their earlier policy, now be willing to discuss the issue of sovereignty. In fact, during a discussion in the British House of Commons, this issue was raised, and the British prime minister indicated that Britain had agreed to discuss anything.

Another objection focused on the fact that Spain had agreed to lift only current measures in force, but nothing banned Spain from reimposing any and all sanctions at any time it desired. Gibraltarians also suspected that Spain had only raised the issue of the lifting of restrictions, because it needed British support to become a member of the EC and to eliminate the protests against this policy by Spaniards living near Gibraltar, who might overwhelm the city looking for work if the border opened.

As it turned out, neither the new cordiality nor the Lisbon Agreement provided a basis for resolution of the situation. When the border was not reopened by June 1, 1980, both sides insisted that the delay was caused by technical issues. Further discussions produced a serious problem, however, as London and Madrid disagreed over the interpretation of the third clause.

In other international developments, despite Great Britain's support, it looked as though Spain's entry into the EC would be delayed, largely because of French opposition. In light of this new situation, Spain wanted specific guarantees in its resolution of the Gibraltar issue that would prevent discrimination and ensure that Spaniards would be able to live and work in Gibraltar until Spain was formally admitted to the EC. Britain, as well as the population of Gibraltar, insisted that the granting of rights to Spaniards could not occur until after the borders had been opened. Anglo-Spanish talks in 1981 did not open under favorable conditions, and Spain had internal problems as well. Growing concerns about the stability of democracy in Spain further weakened its application to the EC but actually hastened its application to NATO because of the view that Spain's membership in NATO was likely to strengthen its democracy.

Spain's application to NATO provided the impetus to break the impasse in Anglo-Spanish relations. Spain became a member of NATO in 1982, and at a NATO meeting held in Brussels on December 9–10 of that year, the British and Spanish representatives scheduled discussions on reopening the border in 1983. Despite continuing differences, the discussions produced an agreement between the two countries during a meeting in

Brussels in 1984. The Brussels Agreement clarified the Lisbon Agreement and provided terms for the lifting of border restrictions, which were an obstacle to Spain's entry to the European Community.

This agreement essentially required that Britain allow Spaniards to live and work in Gibraltar and it required Spain to lift the border restrictions. These concessions were hardly significant, as they would have automatically been required and come into effect as soon as Spain formally became a member of the EC. Following the agreement, on February 4–5, 1985, the border between Spain and Gibraltar was reopened for the first time since the partial restrictions were imposed by Franco in 1964, and complete freedom of movement and communication between the two territories were allowed. A few days prior to the border opening, the dockyard was converted from a naval base to a shipyard repair dock. The population of Gibraltar objected to the Brussels Agreement, however, and continued to oppose it, even after the lifting of the restrictions.

The election in Gibraltar in 1998 resulted in a socialist victory and a departure from traditional politics in Gibraltar. The population was reacting to the Brussels Agreement of 1984 and also to the perceived threat resulting from closer cooperation between Britain and Spain, which had worked out the dispute over air space and set up flights between the two territories. Discussions continued, and relations fluctuated between being friendly and less friendly, but the details of all of the meetings and notes are ultimately less important than the fact that the fundamental issues remained unresolved.

The British were willing to support Spain to a far greater extent than in earlier periods but were unwilling to flagrantly violate the expressed wishes of Gibraltarians by transferring sovereignty to Spain. The population of Gibraltar remained adamant in its desire to remain associated with Britain, and Spain continued to insist that its territorial integrity was and continued to be violated as long as Gibraltar remained separate. In 2004, Britain and Spain agreed to allow Gibraltarian representation at talks to resolve Gibraltar's future. It was a promising sign, but because previous agreements and increased cooperation did not resolve the question of Gibraltar between 1704 and 2006, one should by no means assume that a resolution to the dispute is within sight.

8

Conclusions

The unification of Spain under a powerful monarchy (a process completed in 1462), the conquest of Gibraltar, and the expulsion of Jews and Moors (however racially motivated, originally) are intrinsically linked in the mind of Spaniards. Gibraltar became the symbol of Spanish national and religious unity, and Queen Isabella designated it as "the key to Spain." Therefore, its conquest by Britain in 1704 was viewed as far more than a military defeat and the loss of territory. It was seen as a national affront, as well as the destruction of the territorial integrity of Spain.

The British viewed the conquest in a more practical manner. Gibraltar was strategically valuable for its position at the entrance to the Mediterranean Sea, although virtually all supplies had to be provided and transported to Gibraltar and the supply lines were made extremely vulnerable by their proximity to a deeply embittered Spanish nation. Neither side was entirely convinced that Gibraltar would remain a British possession, yet it has remained linked to Great Britain through the beginning of the twenty-first century. A more complex and startling aspect of the dispute over Gibraltar is the fact that there has been no official border since the conquest of "the Rock" in 1704.

A multitude of issues emerged with regard to Gibraltar, and endless notes were exchanged between Spain and England. The fundamental nature of the dispute, however, can be summarized as follows: The Treaty of Peace and Friendship, which ceded Gibraltar to Great Britain, was the result of an intense and lengthy negotiation, but the final version had several vague and unclear phrases and failed to delineate an exact border on land or at sea. The relevant clauses have been discussed at length in earlier chapters, but it is worth noting again that, in an attempt to prevent smuggling, the treaty clearly stated that no territorial jurisdiction is ceded nor any open communication by land with the Spanish mainland. Spain has at times enforced the literal meaning of the paragraph, stating that no territorial jurisdiction is granted to the British and has ignored the paragraph immediately following, which states that, in order to make up for the lack of territorial jurisdiction, provisions will be provided from the adjoining territory.[102]

The failure to indicate exact jurisdiction has increased the bitterness of the dispute. The ability of the British to occupy land clearly not ceded to them by the treaty has infuriated the Spanish, whereas the Spanish refusal to allow the British to assist their own ships in trouble in waters claimed by Spain has enraged the British. Furthermore, there can be no border more arbitrary than one that does not actually exist. The border between Spain and Gibraltar has never been an actual line of demarcation. Spain's constant refusal to recognize the border, and its partial and complete closing of the border during periods of conflict or diplomatic disputes, further contributed to the arbitrary nature of the border.

Both the British and Spanish have flagrantly violated the terms of the treaty. Spain insists that the treaty is null and void because of British violations, but Spain does not acknowledge its own violations. The central issue is not a breach of contract but rather a breach of ownership and acquisition of territory. The British insist that they acquired Gibraltar and sovereignty over it by conquering it, and that the treaty was merely a formality. Spain, contradicting itself, on the one hand, insists that neither Britain's military conquest of Gibraltar nor the treaty give Britain a legitimate claim to the territory, but, on the other hand, that Britain's claim to sovereignty is based solely on the treaty, and thus if the British violate the treaty, they also nullify their right to possess Gibraltar.

Spain has denounced the population of Gibraltar and questioned the moral character of the inhabitants since the territory's conquest by the British. The questions raised about the nature of the population on Gibraltar took on a new significance in the aftermath of World War II, when Britain freely admitted to the United Nations that Gibraltar was a dependent or non-self-governing territory and agreed to submit reports. When Britain, as a result of pressure from Gibraltarians, instituted changes that gave Gibraltar a greater measure of independence, Spain protested.

Britain might have expected the United Nations—with its clear statements on the necessity and desirability of independence for colonial territories—to support its position. The UN Special Committee of 24 on Decolonization found Spain's arguments—that the population of Gibraltar consisted of British military personnel and displaced British citizens—compelling. The UN agreed that a dispute existed between Spain and Britain over Gibraltar and advised the two countries to resolve the matter through direct negotiations.

The population of Gibraltar, however, did not accept the UN ruling and insisted that it wanted to remain connected to Britain. It is ironic that, at the end of World War II, tensions between Britain and the population of Gibraltar reached their high point and that this was probably the best opportunity Spain had since the loss of "the Rock" in 1704 to regain it. It is also ironic that the actions taken by Francisco Franco and Spain completely destroyed any potential for winning over the population and gaining support in either Britain or Gibraltar for the transfer of sovereignty to Spain. The border had been extremely arbitrary in the years before and during World War I. During this period, goods and individuals had freely passed between Gibraltar and Spain and the populations of the two territories had been closely linked. This natural tendency of the two populations to interact demonstrated the artificial division that had been created and continued to exist so long as Britain retained possession of Gibraltar.

Franco did not introduce any measures that increased trade and benefited the population of Gibraltar, nor did he try to use resentment over issues such as the forced evacuation and long-delayed return of Gibraltarians to increase anti-British sentiments. Instead, he demanded the immediate return of Gibraltar, initiated a newspaper campaign in which the entire population was characterized as criminals and individuals of dubious moral character, and imposed border restrictions that caused real hardships on the inhabitants.

It is impossible to discern why Franco thought he could force the British to hand over Gibraltar by imposing border restrictions. Franco had successfully outmaneuvered Hitler and kept Spain out of the war, despite significant pressure from Germany, and he had watched Britain vow to continue fighting when it had no allies and knew it must face the Nazi war machine that had defeated Poland and France.

It seems incredible that Franco thought that Britain, which faced Germany alone, would give in and transfer Gibraltar to Spain if Spain imposed sanctions on travel and trade between Gibraltar and Spain. As a result of the policies implemented by Franco, however, the British refused to negotiate with Spain on any issue relating to Gibraltar until all border restrictions had been lifted. Britain was also both compelled and far more willing to vote for the approval of large sums of money to subsidize Gibraltar and to sustain and improve the standard of living there, as long as Spain continued such actions. Franco had unified the British and the Gibraltarians against Spain, and the previous grievances on both sides were unimportant in light of such larger issues.

Franco had misjudged Spain and Gibraltarians, and he had virtually guaranteed that the inhabitants of Gibraltar would insist on remaining linked to Britain. Not even the startling announcement by the Spanish foreign minister (that Spain would prefer to look not to the past and to the Treaty of Utrecht, but to seek a solution in the present), nor the death of Franco, nor the implementation of democracy in Spain could alter the fundamental nature of the dispute.

Spain insists that its territorial integrity was compromised by the seizure of Gibraltar and that, as a part of the decolonization process, this territory should be returned to Spain. Britain maintains that the most important issue in regard to the decolonization or the granting of independence to a territory should be the expressed wishes of the population. There is no question in regard to the wishes of Gibraltarians. They sent delegates to the UN meetings to make clear their desire to remain linked to Britain and voted overwhelmingly in the referendum of 1967 to remain so, thus rejecting the idea that

partial or full sovereignty over the territory should be transferred to Spain.

The former British Foreign Secretary Lord Carrington is
quoted as having said that, "the problem for Spain is that
Gibraltar is in Europe."[103] Carrington suggests that if Gibraltar
were not in Europe, the matter would be settled in the same
manner as Hong Kong or other colonial territories, and the territory would become independent. This quote is very sugges-
tive. On the one hand, it suggests that, as the European
community becomes stronger, Britain, which has been more
flexible in terms of discussing issues with Spain, would allow
Spain to claim the territory as long as the rights of the population are guaranteed.

The population of Gibraltar is adamantly opposed to any
transfer, whether real or symbolic, of sovereignty over the territory, and because the inhabitants are primarily Europeans who
emigrated from Britain, Italy, Spain, and other parts of the continent, Britain is unwilling to blatantly violate their expressed
wishes. Even if Britain is basing its policy on Gibraltar on the
assumption that it is part of the Iberian Peninsula and thus in
Europe, it seems to support Spain's argument that the territorial
integrity of Spain has been violated by British possession of "the
Rock."

At several different times between 1704 and 2004, Spain
attempted to seize Gibraltar by force. Spain also engaged in
extensive diplomatic negotiations designed to secure the return
of the "key to Spain." Britain maintained Gibraltar initially
because no satisfactory arrangement could be made; later
because of the British public's attachment to "the Rock" after the
Great Siege; and in the aftermath of World War II, because the
population requested that it do so. Spain refuses to recognize a
border or the British right to sovereignty; Britain refuses to
negotiate on the issue of sovereignty; and Gibraltarians refuse to
consider any alternative that includes active participation by
Spain. Relations between Spain and Britain have only improved
during periods when the issue of Gibraltar has been ignored or

Although Gibraltar is a member of the European Union, it enjoys a number of dispensations; one of the most important of which is that it does not have to tender any of its customs revenue to the EU. Pictured here are Gibraltarians who are protesting outside the EU's headquarters in Brussels, Belgium, to voice their concern over Spain's campaign to block their economic freedoms.

when additional vaguely worded agreements have been suggested or approved.

Works by several historians have ended on a note of optimism, suggesting that improved relations between Spain and

Britain signified a new opportunity to reach an agreement. Both countries issued a joint statement in 2004 stating that the future status of Gibraltar must take into account the wishes of the population. The declaration signifies a renewed attempt at cooperation, but the words are merely words, and in more than 300 years of discussions and diplomatic exchanges, words have not been able to resolve the insoluble problem. Moreover, the artificial division between Gibraltar and Spain became real between 1969 and 1985, when the border was completely sealed. The population of Gibraltar, out of necessity and out of outrage over Spain's closing of the border, forged much closer ties to Britain. As a result, Gibraltarians were increasingly loyal to Britain, and their culture to a great extent reflected their strong links to Britain and their lack of contact with Spain after Franco transformed the arbitrary border into a real one. Although there is still no official border and the unofficial border has been re-opened, it is far less arbitrary than in any previous period, because there is now a very real divide between the population of Gibraltar and the population of Spain.

950 B.C.	Phoenicians found Carteia.
A.D. 711	Moorish forces led by Tarik Ibn Ziyad settle on Gibraltar.
1462	During the eighth recorded siege, the Spanish succeed in taking Gibraltar on August 29.
1466–1467	The ninth siege results in the capture of "the Rock" by Henry de Guzman, who is the son of the duke of Medina Sidonia.
1502	Gibraltar is formally declared to be under the jurisdiction of the Crown, or monarchy, of Spain.
1700–1714	War of the Spanish Succession breaks out at the death of Charles II, the last Spanish Habsburg king, who willed his possessions (including the Spanish throne) to his grandson Philip V of France.

711
Moors settle on Gibraltar

1502
Gibraltar formally comes
under the jurisdiction
of the Crown of Spain

1869
Gibraltar's importance
increases when
the Suez Canal opens

711   1939

1704
Sir George Rooke
undertakes
the eleventh siege
of Gibraltar

1936–1939
Spanish
Civil War

1462
Spain regains
control
of Gibraltar

1779–1783
The Great
Siege occurs

132

1704 Admiral Sir George Rooke undertakes the eleventh siege of Gibraltar, and an Anglo-Dutch force under his command seizes Gibraltar.

1704–1705 The twelfth, unsuccessful, siege of Gibraltar consists of a combined Franco-Spanish effort to regain "the Rock."

1713 The Treaty of Utrecht consists of several separate treaties, one of which cedes Gibraltar to the British.

1727 The second unsuccessful attempt by Spanish and French forces to take Gibraltar is recorded as the thirteenth siege.

1779–1783 The fourteenth recorded siege of Gibraltar, known as the Great Siege, occurs; the British garrison under General Eliott successfully holds out against a

1954
Spain initiates partial closing between Gibraltar and Spain

1950
British grant Gibraltar its first legislative council

1967
Gibraltarians vote overwhelmingly (99%) to remain a British possession

1985
Last restrictions imposed by Spain along the Spanish-Gibraltar border are lifted

1939 2004

1939–1945
World War II—Axis Powers threaten Gibraltar, and the United States uses "the Rock" as the base of operations for attack on North Africa

1963–1964
Status of Gibraltar addressed by United Nations Special Committee of 24

1969
Britain introduces a new constitution for Gibraltar

2004
Britain and Spain agree to allow Gibraltar to represent itself in a new forum on the territory's future

combined Franco-Spanish effort that lasts for more than three and a half years and increases British determination to retain "the Rock."

1805   Admiral Lord Nelson defeats the Spanish fleet during the naval battle of Trafalgar.

1869   The Suez Canal is opened and increases the significance of Gibraltar, which is used as a coaling station for ships headed to India and the Far East.

1914–1918   Gibraltar serves as a base for refueling and repairs for the British fleet during World War I.

1936–1939   The Spanish Civil War is fought and ultimately won by Francisco Franco, who tries to regain Gibraltar for Spain.

1939–1945   During World War II, Adolf Hitler expresses a desire to seize Gibraltar, and Spain's neutrality and friendly relations with the Axis Powers leads to fears that Gibraltar will be attacked; Axis forces do not launch an attack against "the Rock," however, and Gibraltar is used as a gathering point for Allied convoys and as a base of operations for the Anglo-American attack on North Africa, code-named Operation Torch, in 1942.

1950   The British grant Gibraltar its first legislative council, with voting based on proportional representation; British Prince Philip, Duke of Edinburgh, indicates that Britain's long-term goal is to make Gibraltar self-governing; Franco responds by demanding that Britain return Gibraltar to Spain.

1954   Queen Elizabeth II visits Gibraltar; Spain states that it will comply more strictly with the terms of the Treaty of Utrecht and closes the Spanish consulate on Gibraltar; Spain also prohibits Spanish citizens with no justifiable reason from traveling to Gibraltar.

1955   Spain is admitted to the United Nations.

1963–1964   The United Nations Special Committee of 24 on Decolonization initiates discussions on the status of Gibraltar.

1964   A constitutional conference in Gibraltar results in a greater measure of self-rule for Gibraltarians; a resolution adopted by the United Nations urges Spain and Britain to try and resolve the status of Gibraltar through diplomatic negotiations; Francisco Franco of Spain denounces British actions in regard to Gibraltar and institutes measures that increase in severity over the next five years, restricting trade and travel between Spain and Gibraltar.

1966 Because of the influence of the UN General Assembly, Anglo-Spanish negotiations in regard to "the Rock" resume; on May 18, 1966, Spain offers Gibraltar the right to democratic self-government and the right of residence, which would be guaranteed by an international committee on the condition that sovereignty over the territory be ceded to Spain; Britain ignores the Spanish proposal and requests that the dispute over Gibraltar be submitted to the International Court at the Hague for settlement; Spain responds by implementing further border restrictions.

1967 Despite opposition by Spain and the United Nations, the British hold a referendum on Gibraltar, asking the inhabitants whether they prefer to remain a British possession or to be transferred to Spanish jurisdiction; they vote overwhelmingly (99 percent) to remain a British possession.

1969 Britain introduces a new constitution for Gibraltar, which grants full internal self-government to Gibraltar but reaffirms its connection to Britain; Spain responds by closing its border with Gibraltar, withdrawing its labor force, and cutting transportation and communication links.

1973 Britain joins the European Economic Community (EEC), and Gibraltar also becomes a part of the EEC because of its status as a British dependent territory.

1975 General Francisco Franco dies, and Spain comes under the leadership of King Juan Carlos, who establishes democratic institutions.

1980 Spain and Britain sign the Lisbon Agreement, which states that the border between Gibraltar and Spain should be reopened.

1981 The population of Gibraltar is granted full British citizenship.

1984 Under the terms of the Brussels Agreement, England and Spain try to resolve differences over Gibraltar; free travel between Spain and Gibraltar is restored, and Britain agrees to provide equal rights for Spaniards in Gibraltar, whereas Spain agrees to provide equal rights for Gibraltarians in Spain.

1985 The last of the restrictions imposed by Spain along the Spanish-Gibraltar border are lifted; negotiations in regard to Gibraltar continue.

2004 British defense secretary visits Gibraltar, an act criticized by Madrid; Britain and Spain, in a new forum on the territory's future, agree to allow Gibraltar to represent itself.

Chapter 1

1. D. S. Morris and R. H. Haigh, *Britain, Spain and Gibraltar 1945–1990: The Eternal Triangle.* New York: Routledge, 1992, p. 5.
2. Peter Gold, *Gibraltar: British or Spanish?* New York: Routledge, 2005, pp. 6–7.
3. George Hills, *Rock of Contention: A History of Gibraltar.* London: Robert Hale and Company, 1974, p. 222.
4. C. E. Carrington, *Gibraltar.* London: Oxford University Press, 1956, p. 2.
5. Philip Dennis, *Gibraltar and Its People.* London: David and Charles, 1990, pp. 80–81.
6. Peter Gold, *Gibraltar*, p. 6.
7. A.B.M. Serfaty, *The Jews of Gibraltar Under British Rule.* Gibraltar: Beanland, Malin & Co. 1933, p. 5.
8. Dennis, *Gibraltar*, pp. 84–85.
9. Morris and Haigh, *Britain, Spain and Gibraltar*, pp. 32–33.
10. Anja Kellermann, *A New New English: Language, Politics, and Identity in Gibraltar.* Heidelberg: Herstellung, 2001, p. 1.
11. Morris and Haigh, *Britain, Spain and Gibraltar*, pp. 32–33.
12. Norman Ho, "A Rocky Road: The Political Fate of Gibraltar," *Harvard Review* 25, i4 (Winter 2004), pp. 80–81.

Chapter 2

13. Graham Shields, *Gibraltar*, World Bibliographical Series, Vol. 87. Oxford: Clio Press, 1987, p. xxiv.
14. Scott C. Truver, *The Strait of Gibraltar and the Mediterranean.* Germantown, Md.: Sijthoff & Noordhoff, 1980, pp. 160–61.
15. Allen Andrews. *Proud Fortress: The Fighting Story of Tobruk.* London: Evans Brothers, 1958, p. 14.
16. Ibid.
17. Truver, p. 160.
18. Howard S. Levie, *The Status of Gibraltar.* Boulder, Colo.: Westview Press, 1983, p. 3.
19. Jose Carlos de Luna, *Gibraltar in War, Diplomacy and Politics.* Madrid: Publicaciones Espanolas, 1952, p. 4.
20. Ernle Bradford, *Gibraltar.* London: Rupert Hart-Davis, 1971, p. 11.
21. Levie, *The Status of Gibraltar*, pp. 3, 143.
22. R. Dykes Shaw, "The Fall of the Visigothic Power in Spain," *The English Historical Review*, 21, 82 (April, 1906), p. 222.
23. Levie, *The Status of Gibraltar*, pp. 3, 4, 143.
24. Shields, *Gibraltar*, p. xii.
25. Ibid., p. xiii.
26. de Luna, *Gibraltar in War*, p. 24.
27. Bradford, *Gibraltar*, pp. 42–46.
28. Sir William G. F. Jackson, *The Rock of the Gibraltarians: A History of Gibraltar.* London: Associated University Presses, 1987, pp. 96–98.
29. Ibid.
30. John David Stewart, *Gibraltar: The Keystone.* Boston: Houghton Mifflin, 1967, pp. 91–92.
31. de Luna, *Gibraltar in War*, pp. 37–38.
32. George Hills, *Rock of Contention: A History of Gibraltar*, pp. 475–477.
33. Ibid., p. 475.
34. W. F. Monk, *Britain in the Western Mediterranean.* London: William Brendan, 1953, pp. 38–39.
35. Hills, *Rock of Contention*, p. 219.
36. Ibid., p. 219.

Chapter 3

37. Ibid, pp. 219–220.
38. Carrington, *Gibraltar*, p. 11.
39. Levie, *The Status of Gibraltar*, pp. 25–30.
40. Jackson, *The Rock of the Gibraltarians*, pp. 115–116.
41. G. T. Garratt, *Gibraltar and the Mediterranean.* London: Johathan Cape, 1939, pp. 56–58.
42. Ibid.
43. Ibid., p. 59.
44. Dennis, *Gibraltar*, pp. 102–104.
45. Tom Henderson McGuffie, *The Siege of Gibraltar, 1779–1783.* London: B. T. Batsford, 1965, pp. 36–43.
46. Ibid., pp. 63–67, 85–86, 150–158.
47. Dennis, *Gibraltar*, pp. 102–104.
48. Wilbur C. Abbott, *An Introduction to the Documents Relating to the International Status of Gibraltar 1704–1934.* New York: Macmillan, 1934, p. 15, and Frederick Harris, *Gibraltar: A Case Study of the Conflict Between the Sovereign Rights of a State and the Principle of Self-Determination.*

Ph.D. dissertation, New School for Social Research, 1979, pp. 62–65.

49. Garratt, *Gibraltar*, pp. 104–105.
50. Ibid., p. 107.
51. Kellermann, *A New New English*, pp. 23–24.
52. Harris, *Gibraltar*, pp. 68–69.
53. Harris, *Gibraltar*, p. 69.

Chapter 4

54. Quoted in Kellermann, *A New New English*, p. 13.
55. Ibid., pp. 25–27.
56. Ibid.
57. *Documents on Gibraltar: Gibraltar in the Spanish Cortes*. Document #9. Madrid: Government Printing Office, 1965, pp. 174–182.
58. Carrington, *Gibraltar*, p. 23.
59. Ibid., pp. 22–24.
60. Ibid.
61. Hills, *Rock of Contention*, pp. 376–377.
62. Ibid.
63. Garratt, *Gibraltar*, p. 130.
64. Hills, *Rock of Contention*, p. 379.
65. Bradford, *Gibraltar*, pp. 150–154.
66. Ibid., p. 152.
67. Ibid., p. 158.
68. Harris, *Gibraltar*, p. 81.
69. Ibid, pp. 86–87.
70. Ibid.
71. Hills, *Rock of Contention*, pp. 398–404.

Chapter 5

72. J. B. Greaves, Department of Overseas Trade, *Report on Economic Conditions in Cyprus and Malta; With a Note on the Trade of Gibraltar*. London: His Majesty's Stationary Office, 1935, pp. 70–71.
73. Harris, *Gibraltar*, pp. 89–92.
74. Ibid., pp. 89–92.
75. Hills, *Rock of Contention*, pp. 420–421.
76. Ibid.
77. Winston Churchill, *The Second World War*, Vol. II. Boston: Houghton Mifflin, 1949, p. 519.
78. Ibid.
79. Norman J. W. Goda, "The Riddle of the Rock: A Reassessment of German Motives for the Capture of Gibraltar in the Second World War." *Journal of Contemporary History* 28, no. 2 (April 1993): pp. 297–314.
80. Hills, *Rock of Contention*, pp. 428–429.
81. Goda, "The Riddle of the Rock," pp. 297–314.
82. Ibid.
83. Hills, *Rock of Contention*, pp. 428–432.
84. Winston Churchill, *The Second World War*, Vol. IV. Boston: Houghton Mifflin, 1950, pp. 528–529.

Chapter 6

85. Harris, *Gibraltar*, pp. 99–101.
86. Bradford, *Gibraltar*, p. 198.
87. Peter Gold, *A Stone in Spain's Shoe: The Search for a Solution to the Problem of Gibraltar*. Liverpool, UK: Liverpool University Press, 1994, p. 214.
88. Hills, *Rock of Contention*, p. 442.
89. Harris, *Gibraltar*, p. 102.
90. Morris and Haigh, *Britain, Spain and Gibraltar*, pp. 10–14.
91. Hills, *Rock of Contention*, p. 449.
92. Harris, *Gibraltar*, pp. 158–159.
93. A full text version of UN Resolution 1514 (XV), which was passed at the 947th plenary meeting, December 14, 1960, can be found on the following Web site: *http://gibnet.comtexts/un1514/htm*. See also, Harris, *Gibraltar*, Appendix B, 434–436.
94. For a further discussion regarding the population of Gibraltar and other topics related to the issues raised during discussions at the United Nations, see Levie, *The Status of Gibraltar*, pp. 93–105.
95. A facsimile of Resolution 1541 (XV), "Principles which should guide Members in determining whether or not an obligation exists to transmit information called for under Article 73e of the Charter," can be found online at the following Web site *http://www.un.org/Depts/dpi/decolonialization/docs.htm*.
96. Ibid.
97. Hills, *Rock of Contention*, p. 452.
98. Morris and Haigh, *Britain, Spain and Gibraltar*, p. 23–24.
99. Ibid., p. 45.

100. Gold, *Gibraltar: British or Spanish?*, p. 22.
101. Morris and Haigh, *Britain, Spain and Gibraltar*, pp. 78–79.

Chapter 8

102. Hills, *Rock of Contention*, pp. 222–223.
103. Gold, *Gibraltar: British or Spanish?*, p. 4.

Abbott, Wilbur C. *An Introduction to the Documents Relating to the International Status of Gibraltar 1704–1934*. New York: Macmillan, 1934.

Bradford, Ernle. *Gibraltar: The History of Fortress*. New York: Harcourt Brace Jovanovich, 1971.

Butler, M., and J.M.A. Gwyer. *History of the Second World War: Grand Strategy*. Vol. III. London: Her Majesty's Stationery Office, 1964.

Carrington, C. E. *Gibraltar*. London: Royal Institute of International Affairs, Oxford University Press, 1958.

Churchill, Winston S. *The Hinge of Fate*. Boston: Houghton Mifflin, 1950.

——. *Their Finest Hour*. Boston: Houghton Mifflin, 1949.

Dennis, Philip. *Gibraltar and Its People*. London: David and Charles, 1990.

——. *Gibraltar*. The Island Series. Devon, UK: David and Charles, 1977.

Documents on Gibraltar. Presented to the Spanish Cortes by the Minister of Foreign Affairs. Madrid, 1965.

Garratt, G. T. *Gibraltar and the Mediterranean*. London: Johathan Cape, 1939.

Goda, Norman J. W. "The Riddle of the Rock: A Reassessment of German Motives for the Capture of Gibraltar in the Second World War." *Journal of Contemporary History* 28, no. 2 (April 1993): pp. 297–314.

Gold, Peter. *A Stone in Spain's Shoe: The Search for a Solution to the Problem of Gibraltar*. Liverpool, UK: Liverpool University Press, 1994.

——. *Gibraltar: British or Spanish?* London: Routledge, 2005.

Greaves, J. B. *Department of Overseas Trade Report on Economic Conditions in Cyprus and Malta: With a Note on the Trade of Gibraltar*. London: His Majesty's Stationery Office, 1935.

Harris, Frederick B. *Gibraltar: A Case Study of the Conflict Between the Sovereign Rights of a State and the Principle of Self-Determination*. Ph.D. dissertation, New School for Social Research, 1978.

Hills, George. *Rock of Contention*. London: Robert Hale, 1974.

Jackson, W. G. F. *The Rock of the Gibraltarians*. Rutherford, N.J.: Farleigh Dickinson University Press, 1987.

Kellermann, Anja. *A New New English: Language, Politics, and Identity in Gibraltar*. Heidelberg: Herstellung, 2001.

Kenyon, E. R. *Gibraltar Under Moor, Spaniard and Briton*. London: Methuen, 1938.

Levie, Howard S. *The Status of Gibraltar*. Boulder, Colo.: Westview Press, 1983.

de Luna, Jose Carlos. *Gibraltar in War, Diplomacy and Politics*. Madrid: Publicaciones Espanolas, 1952.

Mahan, A. T. *Influence of Sea Power Upon the French Revolution and Empire*. London: Sampson Low, Marston & Co., 1890.

McGuffie, T. H. *The Siege of Gibraltar 1779–1783*. London: B. T. Batsford, 1965.

Monk, W. F. *Britain in the Western Mediterranean*. London: William Brendon, 1953.

Morris, D. S., and R. H. Haigh. *Britain, Spain and Gibraltar 1945–1990*. London and New York: Routledge, 1992.

Serfaty, A.B.M. *The Jews of Gibraltar Under British Rule*. Gibraltar Beanland, Malin & Co., 1933.

Shaw, R. Dykes. "The Fall of Visigothic Power in Spain." *The English Historical Review* 21, no. 82 (April 1906), 209–228.

Shields, Graham. *Gibraltar.* World Bibliographical Series, Vol. 87. Oxford: Clio Press, 1987.

Stewart, John D. *Gibraltar: The Keystone.* Boston: Houghton Mifflin, 1967.

Truver, Scott C. *The Strait of Gibraltar and the Mediterranean.* Germantown, Md.: Sijthoff & Noordhoff, 1980.

Carrington, C. E. *Gibraltar.* London: Royal Institute of International Affairs, Oxford University Press, 1958.

Dennis, Philip. *Gibraltar and Its People.* London: David and Charles, 1990.

Garratt, G. T. *Gibraltar and the Mediterranean.* London: Johathan Cape, 1939.

Gold, Peter. *Gibraltar: British or Spanish?* London: Routledge, 2005.

Harris, Frederick B. *Gibraltar: A Case Study of the Conflict Between the Sovereign Rights of a State and the Principle of Self-Determination.* Ph.D. dissertation, New School for Social Research, 1978.

Hills, George. *Rock of Contention.* London: Robert Hale, 1974.

Jackson, W. G. F. *The Rock of the Gibraltarians.* Rutherford, N.J.: Farleigh Dickinson University Press, 1987.

Levie, Howard S. *The Status of Gibraltar.* Boulder, Colo.: Westview Press, 1983.

de Luna, Jose Carlos. *Gibraltar in War, Diplomacy and Politics.* Madrid: Publicaciones Espanolas, 1952.

Morris, D. S., and R. H. Haigh. *Britain, Spain and Gibraltar 1945–1990.* London and New York: Routledge, 1992.

Stewart, John D. *Gibraltar.* Boston: Houghton Mifflin, 1967.

Melissa R. Jordine is assistant professor of history at California State University, Fresno. Her primary field of research is Germany and World War II, and she has presented a number of papers related to this subject. Jordine has written encyclopedia entries on European diplomatic history, the Soviet Union, and the cold war. She is the faculty advisor for both the History Project @ Fresno State and the Fresno State Chapter of Phi Alpha Theta, the History Honors Society.

James I. Matray is professor and chair of the History Department at California State University, Chico. He has published more than 40 articles and book chapters on U.S.–Korean relations during and after World War II. Author of *The Reluctant Crusade: American Foreign Policy in Korea, 1941–1950* and *Japan's Emergence as a Global Power,* his most recent publication is *East Asia and the United States: An Encyclopedia of Relations Since 1784.* Matray is also international columnist for the *Donga Ilbo* in South Korea.

George J. Mitchell served as chair of the peace negotiations in Northern Ireland during the 1990s. Under his leadership, a historic accord ending decades of conflict was agreed to by the governments of Ireland and the United Kingdom and the political parties in Northern Ireland. In May 1998, the agreement was overwhelmingly endorsed by a referendum of the voters of Ireland, North and South. Mitchell's leadership earned him worldwide praise and a Nobel Peace Prize nomination. He accepted his appointment to the U.S. Senate in 1980. After leaving the Senate, Senator Mitchell joined the Washington, D.C., law firm of Piper Rudnick, where he now practices law. Senator Mitchell's life and career have embodied a deep commitment to public service, and he continues to be active in worldwide peace and disarmament efforts.